CONFESSIONS OF THE OTHER Woman

A Provocative Memoir of Lust, Lies, Faith, and the Powerful Journey to Forgiveness

TIFFANY A. DAVIS

Editor, Bernice Barber

©2020. LAE Publishing Group, LLC.

Published in the United States by LAE Publishing Group, LLC.
Columbia, Maryland 21044

Unless otherwise noted, Scripture quotes are from the NKJV
versions.

ISBN :978-0-578-60355-1

Library of Congress Control Number:2019917891

Printed in the United States of America

Contents

Dedication

To GOD I owe this all to you. None of this belongs to me. Allow them to see more of you and less of me.

I dedicate this book, "Confessions Of The Other Woman, A Provocative Memoir of Lust, Lies, Faith, and the Powerful Journey to Forgiveness", to all the women who are scared to let go, to all of the woman who are looking for love in all the wrong places, and to all of the women who are empty inside.

Love is unconditional when you learn to love yourself. Find your peace and live in it BOLDLY.

To my two boys, Chuck and Damon, I dedicate this to you for always believing in me as your Mom and being huge supporters of my dreams. To my favorite dog, Champ, thank you for protecting me when I couldn't protect myself. I will forever cherish you as son number three.

Always know nothing is too hard for GOD. Trust GOD always, pray always, forgive always and love often.

Sofia, your dreams are a reality waiting to come into fruition... keep writing baby. This is your blueprint. My one piece of key advice I leave you with, is to never accept 'No'! God will make certain that the right person, place, or thing, will provide your YES! Trust Him!

#TiffanyDavisSpeaks

Introduction

I wrote this book because I had experienced Hell and by the grace of God's mercy, He delivered me. When God delivered me, I made a promise to spread the gospel and help save others from burning too. The transparency and truth that I share in the coming pages will help you realize that you are not alone. It will encourage you to no longer suffer in silence. It is also my hope that my sacrifice gives you a new voice…FREEDOM! What I know is that our experiences are not to be kept a secret. This journey is about sharing hope and love. It's about you.

GOD chose me for this battle because he knew that my circle needed strength. GOD showed me that walking through the fire was for Him to save me. You will walk through the fire, but will you walk out of the fire? That's the question, and you get to decide.

Ask yourself if this is the life you expected being the other woman.

What you will learn through your hell is that you are stronger than you appear to be in your weak decisions.

What you will learn on this journey is it's ok not to settle for being the other woman. It's ok not to destroy someone else's home. It's ok to walk away and never look back. And most importantly, it's ok you *love you*.

You will read in this journey how to surrender and submit to GOD and not man. Find yourself and let go of your past. You are no longer a prisoner to your past or in bondage to your self-inflicted hell.

"Confessions of The Other Woman, A Provocative Memoir of Lust, Lies, Faith, and the Powerful Journey to Forgiveness", will set you *FREE*. Welcome to FREEDOM!

Destructively Yoked

Is this what marriage looks like?

July 30, 2005

"I take you as my lawful wedded husband, to have and to hold from this day forward, for better, for worse, for richer or poorer, in sickness and in health, to love, cherish, and to obey, till death us do part, according to GOD's holy ordinance. I have asked GOD's will to allow us to be equally yoked so that our marriage may prosper in Him and not in the two of us. GOD has made us one, and what GOD has joined we will not allow man to destroy."

I am more than grateful to have a husband that has stepped up as a man to be a father to my son and care for him and take him as his own. It's not often that you find a man who's willing to accept the whole package in a relationship, and for this I am grateful and know that I have married the man that's not just for me, but for me and my child.

Jamaica, we are more than ready for the peace and tranquility that you offer us. This water is so beautiful, so amazing, a peace that I will pray into our marriage. The tranquility that we experience, and the love we have shared during our honeymoon has made me love you even more. I never imagined in a million years that I would be married. Several times I was awakened out of my sleep and asked, "Will you be my wife?" Several times I told you, "No", because I waited for this yes to be the right yes. I am looking forward to sharing a lifetime with you. As much as we have enjoyed this vacation, I am excited to get back home to spend the rest of my life with you.

"Hello Dude, I have tried to call you several times, but you have been ignoring me. When you get this message please call me back. I am sure you know who I am, no need to say."

'You have got to be kidding me. There's no way I am listening to a voice mail from another woman to the man I just married. This has to be old. There is no way that this is recent, for the man I just married and as we are just getting back from our honeymoon. Wake me up out of this nightmare. I can't tell him that I heard this. No way will I start my marriage off like this. I can't let him know that I heard this message, because it must be *old. This message had to be way before we were together.'*

"How was work today? How was your day? Anything that you would like to tell me? Anything that I should know about?"

"Why are you asking me all of these questions Tiff? Where is this coming from?"

"Oh, no reason. I am going to get in the shower, I haven't been feeling well these past few days."

"Are you pregnant, you think? Do you want to go to the doctor? I will take you."

"I think maybe it's because of the voicemail I heard on your phone; it's made me sick to my stomach. How in the hell is there a message on your phone about ignoring a woman when we have been married for less than a month? Walk me through this. You do realize that it's still early and I can file for annulment?"

"Listen Tiff, I don't want anyone but you. I married you. I love you. We don't want to start off like this."

"Oh, really? Ok. You're right. I forgive you this time, but there won't be a next time."

October, 2005

'I can't believe this. I am pregnant. Should I tell my husband? I am not sure if this is what I want. I know my husband wants a child, but I am not sure I can do this again. What if this marriage doesn't work, and then I'm stuck with two kids and end up being a single parent? Before I got married, I was a single parent, but there's no way I can let it happen again. Should I tell him? I have to think this through. He would be so excited. This is all he talks about, having a baby, raising a son or daughter. No! I have to tell him. This is what marriage is about and he loves me, so we will always be a family, right? What am I thinking? This will all work out according to GOD's plan, because that's the reason we are married. This isn't about us. This is about GOD. I can't start this marriage off lying, or not telling him something as important as this. GOD, you will always take care of me, right? I don't have anything to worry about because, GOD, you will always be with me. This has me so nervous and sick to my stomach. I know I can do this. I will tell him tonight that I am pregnant. I will buy another test and show him tonight after I take it again. I know there is no reason to be worried because he is my husband, right? I took these vows to make it last forever, until death do us part, and there is

no reason to think otherwise. Well maybe it is, after hearing that voice mail. Tiffany, stop! Stop talking yourself into all of this nonsense and the 'what if's', if you are happily married. You haven't even been in this for a year and you have way too many scenarios playing out in your head. There is no way you can allow yourself to even talk any of this nonsense into existence.'

'Breathe, just breathe. Ok I can do this.'

"Babe, Babe, come here. Guess what? I am pregnant!! We are having a baby!!"

"Are you serious, or are you just playing with me to get my hopes up? You know what this would mean to me if you really are!"

"I am, look, here's the test. Its two lines. You can't possibly believe I would make this up just to try to make you happy? This is not a subject I would lie about."

A few months later, we are here at the doctor to find out what we are expecting, in the hope that we are having a girl. It's a boy.

"Doctor, are you serious? Whew. I thought it was a girl. I felt like it was a girl. I have been nauseous every single day, nonstop, all day. I just knew that those were the signs for a girl. I am excited as this is a blessing, no matter if it's a girl or boy. Thank you. We will see you on June 10th."

June 8, 2006

"Wake up, wake up! I heard something pop. Water is running down my legs. I can't stop it. We have to go fast! Let's go!"

The birth of my second child is one of my greatest accomplishments at this point in my life, but the post-partum is taking over the joy of having my newborn. I can't get my baby to stop crying, and I am not sleeping. This is starting to cause stress in my life, and in my marriage. My husband and I are not engaging in intimacy and I am not in love with myself or my body anymore. All now seems so complicated, while I assumed all of this would be so great.

'How will I recover from this?'

I no longer feel or look sexy. I don't want my husband to touch me and I don't even want to go out of my home. This is so overwhelming and so depressing. I thought I would never get to this point, but this post-partum is real. I am up late at night and early in the morning, working and nursing my son. I have started to look at my husband as if he is poison, and every word he says I can't stand. There has to be a turning point in the joy of having my blessing.

Months have now passed, and I am finally able to start working out, and my son has finally stopped crying. I have gratefully gotten to the point where my mental stability has allowed me get back to my best version of Tiff. I have joined the gym and I am going all in with my health and transformation. I have started working out with a virtual partner and running on the trails alone. I will not allow myself to fall by the wayside because some man wants me pregnant and barefoot. Being married doesn't mean that I must give up my life and forget who I am, and that's exactly what I won't allow to happen any longer.

Men are very complicated creatures and I am now only starting to see this after the first year. I have started to witness

several behaviors that I thought I would not, and ones that I have
been ignoring.

"Hey Dude, this is Christina. I met you and your friend
tonight at the bar. When you get a chance, can you give me a
call?"

*'Am I dreaming again, or is this another message from
another woman? Am I crazy? Is this still happening? I know I
addressed this before. This isn't what love looks like, nor is it
what a marriage looks like. I told him I would not tolerate this
when it happened the first time. Did it ever stop, or was the
pregnancy a distraction from this behavior?'*

"After several incidents your phone continues to go on
voicemail. You have gotten so comfortable with your dishonesty
in our marriage that you are now at the point where you have no
respect, and you think it's ok for you to be in the streets all hours
of the night. How do you think our marriage will survive? We
are living in a fantasy relationship, and this isn't working. I am
working long hours, and taking care of the kids, and you work,
come home, shower and then hang out. We are living in this
500K home and it's a disaster.   Is this what your plan was? To
get me pregnant and leave me with the responsibility of being a
single mother with two boys and sit back and just keep forgiving
you? You have to be kidding me. This nightmare has gone on
way too long. This is the second time in two years that I am
finding voice mails from other women. I will take the blame. I
will allow you to blame me. I got pregnant, I went through post-
partum and, yes, I let myself go. But I'll be damned if I'm going
to continue sitting back and allowing this to keep happening."

*'Tiffany, get your house in order, get your life in order, and
remember who you were before you said, "I do".'*

"I have to sell this house. I am not willing to do this any longer. I am putting the house on the market tomorrow. I have to down grade. These bills are becoming overwhelming and, at this point, I don't see a way for us to overcome this financial disaster that we have all of a sudden created. We are at a point where we don't even have anything but the light bulb in the fridge. I can't allow my kids to live like this any longer. You are more than welcome to come with me, but I will be out of here in the next 30 days. I won't be in this home any longer. It's no good for our marriage, and it's no good for our financial stability."

Just what we needed - a fresh start in a new apartment. Whew, I thought we would never get to this point. A new place, and a place to try this thing called marriage all over again. We've made it to three years, and many more to go. We can make this work. I know the first two years were a challenge. We are now at a good point in our marriage. We've moved out of the home that caused us some financial issues, and we're off to a fresh start again. We will make this all new and put the past behind us.

I never realized moving to a new home could make this feel so different. It's amazing how our financial status could lift such a burden. Downgrading to a cost-efficient place has surely helped our marriage. It's been a few weeks since we had an argument about our financial situation. What took me so long to make that decision? Doesn't really matter that it took that long; what matters is, I finally did.

"I lost my job today Tiff."

"WHAT!? Lost your job? What do you mean? What happened?"

"I know that they have wanted to get rid of my supervisor for a while. This had me stressed out for a while. I didn't even want to tell you, but I knew it would come to this point. This wasn't because of anything that I did to lose it. My supervisor talked to our group over the last few weeks saying that there will be some changes, so I guess I was one of the changes. F--- it. It is what it is. I will file for unemployment and just try to get a job in the meantime. I mean, you know my skill set. I could possibly get another job with another company. Can you put my resume in for me?"

"Wait, what did I just miss here? You get fired and you say F---, I know your skill set. Clearly, I have missed something here. You make six figures. We will be fine. You don't need my money anyway, and besides, when we first got together you told me that I could just help out, and you would take care of the rest. That was before we found you a decent paying job. No way you can expect me to take care of this entire house and these two boys by myself."

'The rent is due. Car payments are due. The utilities and kids' expenses are piling up. Here we are again, with an apartment that we could afford after moving out of the 500K home we couldn't afford. Just when I thought we were in a good place; we are back to the financial disaster again. At this point, he will need to take any job, anywhere. He can't possibly think this is going to work. Yes, again, I took the vows, through it all, but this is not what marriage looks like. The finances are taking over this relationship and I am starting to get in over my head. He hasn't worked in almost six months and it appears that he is ok with this. I have to come up with a plan.'

'So, we just walk around thinking everything is ok, ignoring the fact that I am now married, but actually single? This is what single looks like - taking care of all the bills, going to work, taking care of the kids, taking care of a grown-ass man, working long hours just to keep my sanity, and to keep from going in the house and arguing. No way in hell will I make this marriage last a lifetime like this. Ok, again, I am just thinking too much. I mean, this is just the first job he lost, and maybe he is going through something. Maybe he doesn't know how to regroup after working for two years at a job and then being let go. I just need to breathe, pray and communicate with my husband.'

'Here's a thought, I need a mini vacation, and what better time to take it then now. Norfolk State Homecoming, here I come. I haven't been to homecoming at my college for more than three years. Perfect way to escape this mess I am dealing with at home. I know it won't erase the issues, but what's better than pain being soothed temporarily? Meeting up with my college roommates and old friends will take this situation at home off of my mind for me, so I can come back to regroup later and deal with this.'

Gracefully Broken

W hat an amazing time, after three years, attending my college homecoming! I was able to connect with many that I had not seen in years. It is an absolute must that I continue to go to homecoming. So many faces, and so many relationships that brought back so many different memories. I mean, NSU made me. I spent some of my best years at Norfolk State. How could I miss this?

I'm married and I probably should not have the thoughts that are running through my mind but, whew, what a good time! You know what they say, "What happens at homecoming, stays at homecoming." So many amazing parties to choose from, and we all know that when you come back from homecoming after being away for a few years, so many men are after you - the ones you've been with already, the ones you were thinking about being with, and the one you actually end up with that weekend. There's no need in coming back to homecoming if you are not there to shine and make them want you, and drool. We all know when it's over everyone heads back to their regular lives.

My girlfriends and I party, drink and laugh most of the night, until we decide who we are leaving with. I mean, this is why we come, right? To enjoy ourselves. We are only here for the next 48 hours, until next year. I just have to remember that the pictures I have can't go in my home, or my husband will accuse me of being with every man that walked on the campus at NSU. He has always been so insecure of me going to homecoming. I guess that was a mistake of mine - sharing my experiences with him during pillow talk. Yes, watch what you say during pillow talk. They will always use that against you at some point in the relationship.

Lessons we learn so quickly after the fall. After enjoying my weekend and dancing until my feet were swollen, I am heading back with a clear mind. I can't wait until next year; the hotel is booked already.

"Tiffany, who the f--- is this? Who is this nigga you are hugged up on? This is why you went to homecoming? This is why you raced out of here? You lied. I knew you were going to see some nigga. You think I'm stupid? You out in public at your homecoming, hugged up on some nigga, taking pictures. I know this pretty boy nigga is someone you been sleeping with. You think it's ok to bring pictures in here, in our home, something we have together? You do realize this is cheating, bitch?"

Wow, not what I expected to come back home to. I totally forgot that I took pictures with so many people that I haven't seen in years. These pictures were all innocent, nothing more than seeing friends from college and wanting to create memories.

'I can't breathe, I can't breathe. What the f--- are you choking me in my sleep for? Are you trying to kill me?'

"Wake up bitch, wake up!"

"Are you crazy? What is going on with you? Don't you ever put your f---ing hands on me. Don't you see our baby boy is in here, sleeping? Are you crazy? What is going on? Why would you choke me in my sleep and try to kill me?"

"Why are you cheating on me with that pretty boy-ass nigga?"

"Is this a joke? Are you serious? This can't be happening. I went to homecoming, enjoyed myself, took pictures with a few friends, and you choke me in my sleep and try to kill me! You have lost your mind! It's three in the morning. You come in here, try to choke me in my sleep over a picture? I know what this is about, and it's not about me taking a picture with someone I went to college with. This is about your insecurities, and I am not dealing with it. You lose your job. I put up with your shit for months. I go out of town to have some time to get my thoughts together, and you accuse me of being with someone I haven't seen in years, a good friend of mine. Isn't it enough that you made sure I didn't have any friends after we got married? Get out, just get out! You better not ever put your f---ing hands on me again, let alone try to choke me in my sleep. You're a f---ing psychopath. If you ever put your hands on me again you better hope you are alive to talk about it!"

"I am sorry Tiff, I don't know what I was thinking when I put my hands on you, when I choked you. I am sorry! We can work through this."

"Why is it always, 'We can work through this?' How many times are we going to work through this before someone ends up dead? You can't keep putting your hands on me when you're upset, because you can't get your shit together. I know what I signed up for, and it damn sure wasn't for someone to put their hands on me like that."

"Tiff, I wanted to tell you, when you were out of town, I got a job offer. I am sorry that when you came back this happened.

I took the job, but it's not paying what I was making before. I took it so that we can have more income coming in."

****

'I have to get back to what I know works; this is the only way that this marriage will last. I have to get back into the Word of GOD. This is what I have always known to work. I have been going back and forth with my husband since we got married. Did he go off like that because he is hiding something. Did he go off like that because he is with someone and I am not giving him the attention to find out? No way in hell that a picture would make someone that mad that he chokes me in my sleep and tries to harm me. I mean, I am his wife, right? What happen to the guy that I was with before I said 'I do'? This is all becoming so complicated. I have to pray for my marriage. I have to pray for my husband. I don't know what will happen the next time he gets so angry and chokes me in my sleep. They say if they do it once, they will do it again, right?'

I'm trying to figure out what my next move will be. There is something in my spirit that's telling me my husband is back to his old antics. He starts a new job and every day he is going out after work to have drinks. So, this is how this works. I have a feeling that there's more to this job. He has been at this job less than a month and every day he's out drinking. It's more important for him to be in the streets after work then focusing on his family.

I have to get my mind right. This is all so overwhelming. I know that I didn't sign up for this and I have said this so many times. I need to figure out why I got married? What is this really about? Did I marry him because he showed me what it looked like for him to be a father to my child? Every day I am falling out of love with him. It's obvious that he is also falling out of love with me. The drinking every day is becoming too much and, once again, we are at the crossroads of separation. I have become every name except Tiffany, and it appears that I am repeating myself. No way in hell did I sign up for this and, what's even worse is, I am holding this in. I feel like I am about to explode. I haven't told anyone about what I am going through in my marriage, and this is a nightmare that I continue to get myself into, over and over. How many times will it take for me to get this right? Or, for that matter, for us to get this right? I just don't know what I need to do. I have gone from one job to two jobs, and trying to keep this house afloat, while he is working when he feels like it. I am a full-time engineer and a personal trainer. I had no choice, right? He has shown me that I can't depend on him, so I had to get another source of income. What in the f--- did I get myself into? This lease is up and I have finally got the nerve to leave him. This isn't going to be easy but it's time for a separation. While the details of what's been going on the last year may seem minimal, they have all be too overwhelming for me to stick with this without counseling.

"Sir, the lease is up once again, and I have found a place. I can't do this with you any longer. You will need to find yourself a place to go to. I am leaving; the kids and I are moving. You can have whatever you want in here; I will start over. I have given all that I can, and I haven't received anything in return. We have turned this marriage into a financial disaster, and you have been doing whatever you want. I choose to no longer be a part of it. I thought about counseling but what will that do? You can go stay where you have been staying while you are hanging out all hours of the night. I will talk to the boys about us splitting up. I am sure they will understand as they are both smart enough to know what's been going on the last year. I can no longer be a part of your past that you never healed. You can choose to stay here, or wherever, but I am leaving. You accused me of cheating multiple times and that couldn't be further from the truth. You have lost a few jobs in the past year and you seem to think that you are entitled for me to take care of you. You are aware that's not how this works. I wish you the best and pray that you can find what you need in the streets where you seem to think your life really is. I get it, though. You came from the streets and you may not think this life is for you. It's hard. I get it. You had to make real life changes, coming from being a street guy, doing the things you did for fast money, to a real life of working for corporate America, to taking care of a family and doing the right thing. Some just won't get it and I guess that's you. I will file the papers for a separation and get them to you."

Navajo Drive - new home again, for the third time, this time without my spouse. How many times have I moved in the last 5 years? How many times have I been separated in the last five years? Does this ever get old? Is this what marriage looks like? I have tried to work this out so many times however, it's just too much. Each time I feel like I am going to lose my mind. The only thing I can do is run from it. This has to be the final time. I can't keep moving my kids each time two adults can't get their lives together. Who am I kidding? Why is it taking me so long to put the divorce papers in? Although it's been peaceful, I am lonely, and my kids are wondering when their Dad will come home. It's kind of hard explaining to them that we will not be getting back together. When we are living together it's hard on them, and when he's gone, it's also hard. How do I make this right? Either way, it's a mess. This is not only destroying me, but also my kids. Should I give this another chance? I mean, we have only been separated three times. Maybe this time it will work. Why am I crazy enough to think I should give him another chance? When we were together, we argued every day, non-stop. Every morning and evening it was the unknown of how bad it would get if we fought or argued. What's going to be the trigger? What will make him mad? What will make me mad? Will he quit his job because something didn't go his way? Will the bills get paid? Of course, they won't because he is mad about something I supposedly did or didn't do. Will I come home to a disaster? Will my kids be scared to go to sleep? By taking him back and letting him move back in, will I be in the same situation I was in three times before? Has he changed? Have I changed? It's only been about six months. Is that really enough time for either one of us to understand what really is going on in this marriage? This marriage thing takes two, so it's not just him, it's the both of us. This is just so stressful. I have work, and I am a personal trainer part-time, training other individuals trying to get their life right, trying to get my life right. Maybe I need to seek counseling. But what is counseling going to do? Who am I kidding? I can't afford that, and I sure as hell don't want my job to know about this chaos. I have a clearance and I can't afford to lose that fighting and arguing with him, and all this nonsense. This is all too much. I never imagined it would all be so complicated. Hell, why in the f--- did I get married anyway? My girlfriends always tell me, 'You knew what this was before you did it. You saw the signs. Did you just ignore it?'

'Tiffany, there you go again, reading way too much into this. You got what you wanted and what you needed for you and your boys. You needed this separation so that you could finally work on you and get your life together after marriage. Isn't this what you really want? Weren't you tired of all of the arguing and

fighting? Weren't you tired of the unknown, of what would be next? Do you really want to wake up every morning to argue, to hear disruption in your home?'

I have to pray on this, I have to seek GOD in this. GOD doesn't approve of divorce.

1 Corinthians 7:39 "A woman is bound to her husband as long as he lives. But if her husband dies, she is free to marry anyone she wishes, but he must belong to the Lord."

So, if I am going to church and I understand the word of GOD, I have to figure out how to make this work. But what I also know, and want to believe is, GOD doesn't want me and my kids to live in this hell also. I understand that marriages aren't perfect, but what I also know is I am not supposed to be living like this either. Who wants to live like this? This shit is crazy. When we are in public, we act like life is good, but as soon as we are alone, all hell breaks out. He seems to think I am living a different life of some sort. He never believes anything I say, and I am always lying about something, according to him. I just have to pray on it and see what's next. Maybe I can start dating him outside of the house to see if this is going to work.

This is all too much. This has given me a headache; I can't even think straight. I have work to do. No way in hell will I allow this to disrupt my employment. I need my job to take care of my kids. My eldest is headed to college in a few years and I have to keep my mind and myself together. I can't allow this to affect my job. No way in hell will that happen.

So here we are, months later. We are back together to try to give this another shot. I have convinced myself to let him come back, another chance for hell to break loose. I can't recall if any of the times were good because, now here we are, in another home. Are we married, or are we just dating, on again, off again? 'Get out' is the new sentence for us when we argue. Throwing a grown man out of the house, or threatening to throw a grown woman out, when she is the bill payer, has now become the new norm for conversations.

What happened in marriage counseling when we were engaged? Did we just show up empty, not listening to each other, or the pastor for that matter? Seven years into this and we are supposed to make it after year five, right? Where are all of these fake narratives about marriage coming from because it sure as hell hasn't worked for me. Where is 'Marriage for Dummies' because, once again, we are back together? This is, 'Split up, separate, then just get back together to see if it will work this time'.

Let me see - here we are in place number four in the last five years. So, I sign a lease for a year because we really don't know how this is going to pan out. Even though we are actually married, every day is a trial, because somewhere love and trust were lost, and we can't seem to figure it out. I need a do-over from year one. No, wait, I need a do-over from the dating, and not marriage.

Who are we? We lost who we were when we said, "I do". I get it, that's what happens. I stopped being Tiffany and he stopped being himself, whoever the f--- that was. It's my hope that letting him back will be different this time. I am not going to hope anything other than that.

"Hey babe, this is a nice spot. How did you find this spot?"

"Yes, I thought it would be good for me and the boys. It is still in the school location for the boys and, of course, my sister lives across the street, which is really convenient for us."

"I bet it's convenient for you, you always run to her for everything."

"I have no choice. When I ask you to do something you always complain, or you don't want to do it."

"Ok, we won't go down that road. We are not going to bring up the past. We are going to be different this time, right? Are you going to let me come and stay with you and the boys so we can work this out?"

"Where are you staying now?"

"Why does all that matter? Are you going to let me come back?"

"Do you have a job?"

"What does that have to do with anything?"

"It has everything to do with it. This was one of our issues. You wouldn't keep a job and I don't want to go back down that road again. I don't want to let you come back and you\re not working, or you won't keep a job."

"Tiffany, who the f--- you think you talking to? You are not my mother."

"See what I mean? Why are you cussing? We have to learn how to talk to each other before we can even think we will be getting back together. You are very disrespectful, and you don't know how to talk to me and the first thing you always say is 'SORRY'. How do you keep saying sorry, but you don't mean it? You don't hear me cussing you, or calling you out of your name, ever. So, back to my question. Are you working, and are you going to help, or is it going to be some 'I don't give a f---.' I can't allow that to happen again. We are going to do this right, or we are not."

"Yes, I have a job and I will do what I can."

"What do you mean, you will do what you can? That's not how this works."

"Tiff, you make good money. You make more than me and you have always made more than me."

"That doesn't matter. This house doesn't run off of 'I won't give' or 'I can give a little here or there'."

"Tiff, why is everything money with you? This is why we can't get along. All you want is my money."

"You can't be serious. You do realize it takes money to run a house, right? You do realize that we have real expenses. Oh, I forgot your usual line will be, 'I am not paying bills and my money is going somewhere else'. You have held on to that line for so long when you've run from responsibilities. Ok, I forgot, this is a conversation about you coming back home, not what happened in the past. I am going to try to not bring up the past because if I do you won't be back, and the papers will already be filed."

"Why the f--- do you always threaten me with filing for a divorce? If that's what you want to do, you need to go ahead and do it, because I am not going to. I am not filing. I want my wife."

"Oh, really? You want your wife, but for some reason it won't work out, so how is it you want your wife? Oh, I did it again. Ok, look let me think about it and I will get back to you."

"Tiff, what is there to think about? You are my wife and they are my kids. This is my family. I don't want anything else."

"Let me get this right. So, we separate for the millionth time, and we never worked on anything while we were separated, but when we apart it was a mess, so you want to try this again? I don't think this is how this is supposed to work. You keep saying you love me. You keep saying this is going to work. Let's take our time, and you stay a few nights at a time."

"Tiff, I don't want to do that. I want to be back with my family. I miss you and my kids."

"Alright. Alright, but this is the last time. I don't want to keep doing this. I am going to pray that this works out, but we will have to go talk to our pastor. We have to figure this out, this isn't healthy for any of us. I will get you a key made, and we can sit down and talk to the kids about what our plans are."

"So, I am going to stay here tonight and then I will get my stuff tomorrow."

"Where do you have to go get your stuff? You can just go get it and if it doesn't work out then we already know what's next. You can just get your stuff tomorrow. But I do want us to go to counseling again with our pastor. I don't want to wait for the next move or the next time one of us will try to kill the other. Each time I feel like we are Mr. And Mrs. Smith.

You do know that movie, don't you? This is what our relationship has been like the entire time. Mr. And Mrs. Smith."

"Why are you always at the gym, Tiff? You spend more time at the gym then you spend with your family. There has to be a nigga at the gym that you are hanging out with, or you're just saying you are going to the gym."

"Oh no, I am definitely not going down this road with you. You have been here less than three months and I have only been in this home six months. No way in hell I am going here with you. You are kidding me, right? We are not about to do this. What I am going to need you to do is get out of my face with this nonsense. I am assuming you are dealing with your own internal issues and you are mad. I am not trying to figure out what is going on with you. Look, I am going to shower and relax."

"So, you just going to act like you not hanging out at the gym with some nigga? And if you not hanging out with him at the gym, he is somewhere you are giving him more time than me."

"Listen dude, I am not going here. Period. I told you. So, whatever you think or feel, do what you need to, but I am not arguing in front of my kids. And I damn sure will not go down this road with you. What is it with you? Why can't you just live? You need help. Every day it's an accusation about something. I sleep here every night. You see me - I work, train others, run kids around to their events, and come home. What the f--- do you do but complain about who or what I am doing. I thought we were going to work this out. We split before for this dumb shit. Have you ever caught me with anyone? No, you seen a picture in a camera from homecoming with friends I went to school with. You have never caught me with a man, nor have you seen any evidence that I was with anyone other than you. I tell you what, until you catch me in the bed, on site, with another man, get the f--- out of my face with this nonsense. I am not going to keep cussing at you about this. Not my character, and I am not going to allow you to make it my character."

"B---, who the f--- you talking to?"

"I am talking to you, and don't call me out of my name again. We did this. Look, I am going to bed. So, you figure this out because I am not waking up to this bullshit in the morning."

I can't believe this, maybe a month without an argument, and now he is back to 'I am with some nigga' talk. This is unreal. Why didn't someone warn me about this, and why do I keep giving him chances? Hell, why does he keep giving me chances at this point? Why are we giving each other chances? Is this so we can kill each other? This shit is starting to be like Mr. and Mrs. Smith. No way in hell am I going to let it get to the point that he may try to kill me in my sleep, or I burn him with hot grits or boil water and stick his hand in it. Nope, not doing that. Yes, you heard me right. Kill, or be killed at this point, because there's no way I will allow a man to put his hands on me. I watched my mother and aunt get beat way too many times. He has already tried to choke me in my sleep. He spat on me several times so, yeah, not going here with him this time. I will just lay low and be his 'yes' woman. That's what will keep him calm. That's what I will do.

'What the hell is wrong with me? Why do I have to keep playing these scenarios out in my head? Why am I planning the next move like this is chess or something?'

I pull up in my driveway, and as soon as I am backing in I have this crazy feeling in my stomach. Before I can get out of my car, this dude with a stack of papers arrives at my car door.

"Tiffany, who the f--- are all these numbers you've been calling? I went to Sprint and got the call log. I called, and some nigga answered the phone."

"Dude, are you ok? Are you crazy? Did you wake up on the wrong side of the bed? You do realize I have been at work, then left work and was training someone today? Do you know what the f--- a job is? You come to my car with phone records. You need to go get checked. Something is seriously wrong with you."

"B-----, get out of the car!"

"Stop talking to me like that. I told you before, you will not call me out of my name. Do you even know what my name is?"

"You heard me, you f---ing slut, get out of the car. Who the f--- are all these numbers?"

"Listen, get away from my car. Don't you see my baby in this car, and you're talking crazy, calling me out of my name."

"B----, you heard me get out of this car. Who are these niggas? I called them. So, you going to tell me or not? You going to make me call them in front of you?"

"Hey, you do what you need to do, but you're the one looking like a jack ass. You do know I have a job, and a side business training?"

"Slut, I bet you do have side training. You are f---ing these niggas. You think I am stupid. All these numbers are not your girlfriends."

"Look, go get you some help and get the f--- away from me. I am not going in my house with this. I don't know what made you go to Sprint to get these phone records, but you might want to get away from me with this. I am not going inside my house with this. We talked about you coming back and not having all this bullshit to go along with it. Why don't you go get help?"

"F--- you Tiffany. Ok, if that's what you want. You are a f---ing slut, you c---."

"Dude, stop talking to me like this. Do you even care that your child is standing right here?"

"He will be ok. He is growing up to be a man."

"Dude, he is five. He is not a man, and he doesn't need to see this mess. You will mess him up."

"I'm not going to do shit. That's my son."

"Ok, ok, you are right. Look, get out of my way, I am going in."

Whew, that was a close call. I thought I was going to have to go on the battlefield without any weapons. Yeah, yeah, you heard right. This dude went to Sprint, got phone records of my call log. I don't know how he was able to do that because we were not on the same plan, but he did. Why? I have no clue. I can assure you, like I did him, I was not stepping out on him. Did I have male friends? Maybe. Was I intimate with them? Hell no. How could I be? He was too crazy, and he was always watching and following me, so even if I wanted to, I didn't. I don't even think I wanted to. I just wanted my life to be right. I just wanted to raise my boys and have a good life, whatever that meant. Take care of my boys, have my marriage work out the way it was supposed to in GOD's eyes, and live a little.

I stopped traveling when I got married, and stopped hanging out with my single girlfriends, so I thought all was well until my spouse started putting all these men on me. Looking back, I could have been a married madam with all the men he accused me of. Now that we have got the Sprint call log out of the way, and I was able to calm him down, I guess I am just waiting for the next Dr. Jekyll / Mr. Hyde incident. I never know which one I am going to get. I don't even know what love looks like, feels like or sounds like at this point. I am such an idiot, I let this dude back and now, not even three months later, we are at each other's throats. I know I just have to be intimate with him; maybe that will calm him down. Maybe I haven't been giving him sex like he wants and that's why he is acting like a fool.

Intimacy was never an issue for us before all of this nonsense started to happen. I mean, who am I kidding? We used to have sex so good, we would flip the mattress. But how can I, when his actions have turned me off? Who wants to be intimate with someone who treats you like shit? The verbal abuse is too much. How am I going to be intimate with a person that uses such language towards me? Cuss me out in one breath, call me every name but Tiffany, then lay down and let him bounce on me, let alone me give him oral sex. Oh well, guess it's something that I have to do, even though I hate it. But at least I will get something out of it. He does have a great tongue though, and I do love sex, so I guess I just might as well calm him down and give him what he wants. I am pretty sure this is one of my reasons for marrying him - the sex was amazing. Give him sex, calm him down and remove the fear that he has about me sleeping with other men.

5:00 a.m. I am sitting in the Harris Teeter parking lot. I just left the gym. For some reason I just can't gather myself to go home. I generally know when my stomach doesn't feel right, something is about to happen. I have been through this so many times. I know he doesn't like for me to go to the gym, and today just feels a little different. No need to sit in this parking lot wondering what's next. I need to get home and get my baby boy off to school. Asking him to get our baby ready for school isn't an option. He will say it's not his responsibility. Every day he talks about how much he hates that I am at the gym because he feels like I am not doing it for me, I am doing it for another man. I have never seen a man that is so obsessed with other men wanting his woman. He has spent most of this time worried about me being with another man. I know he got the phone records from Sprint before, but I can assure you that I have never been caught with another man while married. Like I said before, I could be the married madam with all these men that he has placed me with. Clearly this asshole doesn't like me going to the gym because he thinks I am either after someone in the gym, or someone is after me. I just don't like this feeling. I always trust my gut when it comes to the wild ass dude. I always know when he is ready to go off about something and besides, he was kind of quiet when I left this morning. He is the type to let it grow, then explode. But let him tell me I caused it, or I provoked him to lash out with his verbal abuse, or at any moment I need to be prepared to fight. His favorite line was that I never had my ass beat and I needed it. Who provokes a grown ass man? I always thought grown ass men were in charge of their own actions.

I pull into my garage and I walk into the basement to, "B---, where the f--- have you been? You f---ing slut, you whore! You must think I am stupid."

He snatches my car keys out of my hand, then snatches my phone. He slams me down and we are wrestling. Yes, that is correct, me wrestling for my keys and my phone with this grown ass man.

"Help! Help! Come downstairs boys! Your Dad is attacking me!"

"Shut up B----, close your mouth! You better not yell again!"

"HELP! HELP! BOYS, HELP! Are you f---ing crazy? What is wrong with you? This is exactly why I sat in the parking lot because I knew you would be crazy! Why the f--- did I even let you come back? How could I be so stupid?"

"B----, you been out f---ing some nigga this time of the morning!"

He locks me in the bathroom so I can't get out.

"HELP! HELP! I am calling the police!"

"B----, you are not calling anyone! I am sick of you going out of here every morning, running with some nigga. You must think I am stupid!"

"Dude, you need to calm down! I just came from the gym!"

"Get out this bathroom B----!"

He slams me down on floor again.

"HELP! Boys, come downstairs, your Dad is acting crazy! I don't know who he is. Bring me the phone so I can call the police!"

This jack ass leaves before I get an opportunity to call the police. He races out of the house with my car keys and phone. At this point I am about to lose it because I let this jack ass come back, and I knew it would only be a matter of time before we would fight again, or he would lose his job, or accuse me of being with other men. Well there it was, sooner than I thought.

It was less than six months and he lost his damn mind. In just a few months, he got my phone records, went crazy, locked me in bathroom, and took my keys and phone.

I get the house phone and call the police, only to hear, "Well Ma'am, he is your husband and there is nothing we can do if he took your keys. Technically he is the owner because you are married."

"Are you f---ing kidding me? No way you can come here to tell me some shit like this."

"Ma'am, if he put his hands on you, you can get a warrant."

"But how am I supposed to take my kid to school? He has my phone and keys?"

This shit can't be real. I can't be standing here talking to the police and I have no options because I am married to this jack ass. I don't deserve this shit and my kids definitely don't deserve this. My youngest kid goes in the bathroom while I am talking to the police, and finds my phone in the toilet. Who does this type of shit? A psycho? The real question is, why do I continue to give this psycho a chance, time after time? What is it going to take for me to get that this asshole just can't do the right thing?

'GOD, there is no way that you want me to go through this. I am not perfect GOD, I am not, but I know I don't deserve this. How can this be happening to me? What do I need to do different GOD, or what is it that I am not doing?'

I gave up the life of a single woman, doing what I wanted, to being a faithful, married, abused woman. There has to be a silver lining in this. He is starting to make me think I did cheat. He is starting to make me think I should twist my truth. How am

I sitting here thinking about telling him I am guilty of doing something I have not?

'GOD, HELP me! I am crying out to you! I don't know what else to do.'

Now I am left with no keys and he is starting to cost me more money.

"Dude, answer your phone, I need my car keys. The kids have to go to school. I need to get to work. I have left you several messages. I have called your family. Answer your phone. Call me back. Call the kids, please. You don't have to come back. I just need my keys. Listen, you don't have to call me. You can take the keys to the police station. The police have been called and they are aware of this situation. I know you don't want to be charged with anything so just take the keys to the police station. You don't have to move out; just bring my keys so that I can handle my responsibilities, something that you are not capable of doing. You do realize that these boys need to get to school, and their activities?"

'Tiffany, when are you going to see that this marriage just isn't going to f---ing work? Now this asshole has taken your keys, threw your phone in the toilet, got the phone records, and who knows what else this jack ass has done? Now it's almost a month, and you have been borrowing someone's car because this asshole has left with the keys to the car you are paying for. Don't you see what's going on here? He is trying to paralyze you because he can't control you. Why do you even want to be married to someone like this? Do you realize that he has bigger issues that he hasn't dealt with and he is turning his anger on you? No matter how much you try to love him, care for him, take care of him, or even give him all the sex in the world, you will

never be enough. Tiffany, you have created this monster. It's not going to happen. You have lost control over your marriage and now you are lost trying to explain to your boys why you are stuck in this marriage. You were separated and you were getting your mind together so that you wouldn't be back in this situation, or him in this situation, for that matter. What are you going to do now? How long are you going to wait this asshole out? It's already been more than a month since he disappeared with your keys. You called the police, you called his job, you called his family and you are stuck looking like a fool again because you let him come back. When will it be enough? When you are dead? When he is dead?'

"Mrs. Davis, this is Officer Jones calling from the police department. Your husband has your keys and he would like to meet with us to give them to you, but he doesn't want any problems."

"Are you kidding me? Is this a joke? He wants to meet me with you at my house and he is the one who took the keys to my car and has been gone for over a month. Is this some type of joke? I have a protection order."

"Mrs. Davis, he also has a protection order, so we can meet at your house and give you the keys to your car. Do you have anything of his?"

"I have nothing of his, but I want him out of my home."

"Ma'am, you two share the home and you will have to go to court to get him out. You will have to file for a divorce."

"WHAT!!??" Someone wake me up out of this f---ing nightmare I have been having for years.

'Tiffany, figure out who the f--- you are and get it right. No way do you deserve this and hell, neither does he. Clearly, we do not belong together. We are not good for each other. We are two damaged individuals. Our souls are broken. We are broken human beings that are destroying our kids. Can't you see that you are destroying your children? Wake the f--- up Tiffany and get this right. Your kids will be destroyed, and this will end up having a lasting effect on them.'

I am going to get this right. I am going to fix this situation that's broken. This isn't what marriage looks like and this for damn sure isn't what love looks like.

"Babe, I love you. I want us to work. We can make this work. We have been through a hell storm and back, but we need to make this work for us and, most importantly, for our kids."

"You are kidding me! Our kids? What we will not do is just make this work for our kids. Our kids are smart enough to know what we have been through. You do realize they are two very smart boys?

They have seen us at each other's necks, moving from apartment to apartment, townhouse to townhouse. They do realize that this isn't normal. I can't continue to pretend. This is taking a toll on my health, your health, and both of our mental states. Do you even realize what we have been through? Do you even realize how many times we have split? I don't even know how you could possibly think that this could even work after all the shit we have been through? And again, we are in a new place. The only difference is, this time, I have decided to let you have your name on all of the paperwork and leases, not mine. This is the only thing that's different, but what happens when you lose your mind, or I lose mine for that matter? I don't know how you haven't noticed how this has been. How can we even keep pretending that this is going to work for them? This is not what adults should do. We shouldn't just make this work for the kids, walking around giving fake smiles and love. Do you even realize what we have taken each other and our kids through in the last, I don't even know, how many years? We have been in a nightmare for years. How could you not see this? Let's see, do we need to do a recap of all we have taken each other through, or are we just going to keep pretending that nothing ever happens and we will continue through the hell storm because, clearly, that's what you are used to? This is a generational curse for both of us. This behavior has occurred in your past and in mine and somehow, we are allowing it to affect our kids. I know. I've seen my mother and aunt be verbally and physically abused. Is this why I think that it's ok for you to think you can do to it me? You have apparently seen this in your family, for you to keep telling me that I need my ass beat by a man, and I haven't had an ass-whooping by a man. Who the f--- walks around saying that? When the f--- are you going to go to a counselor to fight the demons that you are fighting in your head, to even say such a thing to someone you supposedly love? I get it. I do. We have mental things we both probably have never dealt with, but for me it's not abuse. I tell you that and what I will tell you is that I will not do this with you. I know the past several years I have said all the other events were the last straw, but what I can tell you is the next fight will be the last fight. No two humans should be going through all of the shit that we have been through, I know that. I can tell you now, we lost GOD after we said, 'I do'. I know that you told me that you loved me, but love is:

1 Corinthians 13:4-5. 'Love suffers long and is kind; love does not envy; love does not parade itself, is not puffed up;

does not behave rudely, does not seek its own, is not provoked, thinks no evil'

Think back over the times up to this moment and you will see it's not love. It was, 'I am here, and I am in lust, or so obsessed with what Tiffany is doing that I lost the path of showing her what love truly is, and how to be the head in the relationship. GOD says man is the head and not the tail, but this isn't it.

Deuteronomy 28:13 "And the LORD shall make thee the head, and not the tail; and thou shalt be above only, and thou shalt not be beneath; if that thou hearken unto commandments of the LORD thy GOD, which I command thee is this day, to observe and to do them."

Lost, just lost. I expected you to be the head always, but somewhere in the disaster it all got lost and you tried way too many times to prove a point that you were a man. When you are a man you don't have to tell someone that you are a man. It shows in your actions that you are a man that takes care of the home and what needs to be taken care of. Abusing your wife and doing the shit that you have done doesn't show a man. It shows you are less than a man. It shows that you are not capable of being the head of the household. Maybe I was too strong and that made you feel some type of way. Maybe me showing you that I was more capable of taking care of the home without you made you feel less and not wanting to do your part. You told me more than once I was acting like the man in the house and I didn't let you take care of what you thought I should have. You wanted to be in charge, but I felt that maybe it wouldn't work because of your past behavior patterns and again, maybe I didn't break the generational cycle that occurred in my family. It's hard when my life has been about working and making it happen. My two boys are always depending on me. They see you in and out, so they don't depend on you, but they know that, no matter what, they have to depend on me. We have to come up with a plan. We need help. We can't do this on our own. I don't know if it's professional help we need, or what, but no way is this going to work if we sweep all this shit under the rug waiting for the next big blow up."

Breaking Point

December 31, 2014

"Tiff, are we going to church tonight? Tiff, I want us to go to church tonight so that we can start fresh for the New Year. I want us to bring in the New Year together with our boys. This is what we need to do as a family."

"No, I am not going to church with you tonight. We have already tried that on New Year's and that didn't work all the past years."

"What you mean, 'No'?"

"Just what I said. I am not going to church with you. I have other plans. I have to go. I am cleaning up."

"Tiffany, what you mean, 'No'?

"Look, I have other plans. I will see you when I get home."

"I may not be here when you get here. I told you I have plans."

"What the f--- do you mean you have plans? See how quickly that turned? One minute you want to go to church to make this work, like you did a quick flick and became someone else. Then you have plans. Look dude, I am hanging up. I have to finish up before I leave. I will talk to you later."

Meanwhile, I am in the house cleaning up trying to get ready for my night out. I had already decided two days ago that I would not be going to church with him, or going to church by myself, or sitting in the house feeling sorry for myself, or anything that I have been going through for that matter. I decided that to bring in the new year, 2015, I would be with my girlfriend that would make me laugh the night away and take the pain of this relationship away. In 2015, my eldest would be graduating from high-school and heading into his next stage of his life. I am creating my exit plan, so what does it matter that I am not bringing in the new year with him? I know that after my eldest graduates from high school, I am out. I am taking my youngest and I am gone for good. I have done this shit more times than I would like to admit, so I am out. I have already packed my bag and I already know where my little one will be. I am going out tonight and hopefully gone before he gets back from work. I can only imagine what will happen if he comes home before I leave to go out. I have put my overnight bag and my clothes for tonight in the car because, if he sees any of that, we will need 911 for sure. It will be a huge fight. In fact, someone might not make it out once he sees my bag. He has already accused me of a million men. Could you imagine if he sees me leaving to go out with a bag?

I am in the house cleaning, running the vacuum, and have already dropped my youngest off with my aunt. As soon as I am finished cleaning up, I can get in the shower and hit the highway. As I finish vacuuming the dining room, I hear, "B---, who the f--- do you think you are? I told you I wanted to go to church. You think you have other plans? You better f---ing cancel them."

"I am not canceling anything, and what you won't be doing is coming in this house talking to me like that. This is the reason that I won't be going to church, or anywhere with you, for that matter. Look, I need to finish this house so you can say and do what you like."

I turn around and this dude is taking my car keys and my purse.

"Wait. wait dude. you can't take my purse or my keys! What the f--- is wrong with you? You don't own me!"

"B----, you not going anywhere today. You don't want to go to church, so you not going anywhere with my car running with some b---- ass nigga on New Year's."

"Give me my purse. Give me my keys!"

I am running out the door and down the stairs, chasing after this asshole that has not only taken the keys to my car that's in his name, but also my purse and the bag that I have packed in the back of the trunk of the car. I am running down the street like a jackass, chasing after him like he is really going to stop and give me my shit back.

This can't be happening to me right now. You mean to tell me that I am chasing behind this asshole that wanted to go to church, and when I say no to him, takes my car, my purse and my belongings that I had packed to go out.

If you recall, I said earlier that I wanted to get out of the house before he came home, because I knew this jack ass would act out because I wasn't giving him his way. Who the f--- wants to deal with this in the new year? Not me. Again, this just helps my exit plans even more. No way am I going to let this ruin my new year, just because I said no to going to church with him. I know he probably thinks because he took the car and my shit I won't be going, but he is wrong. Let me call my girlfriend and my aunt. They are not going to believe this shit. Hell, I can't even believe it, I just feel like I was in a movie. Let me sit and replay this for a moment. You call, want to go to church. I say no. You come home, act like a maniac, take my car, purse, keys and belongings, and then don't answer your phone. What the f--- is this? Whew, ok. I have to gather myself and get out of here before he comes back.

I know he probably thinks that he stopped me, but I will show him.

"Girl, you have to come get me."

"What you mean, I have to come get you? Where is your car? What are you talking about?"

"This dude just lost his mind."

"WHAT!? What you mean he lost his mind? Tiff, I told you that he was crazy. I knew this was going to happen. Shit. Ok, look, are you ok? Are you ok?"

Yes, just meet me in Tyson's. I will get my aunt to bring me. I don't have any money; I don't have anything. He took everything."

"Are you serious? Did he put his hands on you?"

"No, I don't know if that was his intention or not. He wanted me to go to church and I told him I wasn't going to church, and he came in the house while I was cleaning, and he took everything - my clothes that were in the back of the car, everything that I was going to wear tonight, the keys, my purse, wallet. Everything, gone."

"What the f--- is wrong with this dude? You knew his ass was crazy when you married him."

"Look, I don't have time for all of that. I want to still go out."

"So, wait, I am supposed to come get you and buy you shit to wear tonight? Ok, I guess I will dress you up Cinderella. I can't even believe this is happening right now. Alright get your aunt to drop you off, but you better not tell your family what happened, or they will be looking for his ass and you won't be going anywhere."

"I have to tell my aunt, but I will deal with him after I bring in the New Year. See you in a few."

"Hey Auntie, can you come and get me? I am at home."

"What do you mean? I just left there getting your boy. Why do I need to come get and you?"

"I need to you take me to Tyson's. My girlfriend will pick me up from there."

"What happened Tiff? I will kill him if he put his hands on you!"

"He took the car, my purse, and all of my belongings; because I told him I wasn't going to church with him."

"What? Where is he now?"

"I don't know. Just come and get me."

"Perfect! I found the perfect dress! See? This was supposed to happen the way it did. Girl, when I left out of the house, the only tube of lipstick he didn't take, I used to write on the mirror, 'F--- YOU, I am out'. I know he didn't like that. That probably pissed him off more than anything. Two for one - you took my shit, but you didn't stop me from going out. He was probably listening to my conversations and knew that I was going out with you. You know he can't stand you anyway. I always tell him though; no-one can make me do anything that I don't want to do. I am grown and a woman of my own, I make my own decisions, and if I want to sleep with someone else it won't be because my girlfriends make me do it. Men are so simple and have the craziest thoughts when it comes to what someone can make you do. Look, we are not going to worry about him, or anyone else for that matter. What we are going to do is enjoy ourselves tonight and bring this New Year in, in peace and party. I am ready to party. I will deal with him later. I mean, what's the worst? We are only going to fight when I get back home tomorrow because I sure in hell am not returning back home tonight. After I party I am staying at your house and I will go home tomorrow to deal with this bullshit."

"Great! We are going to drink up, honey! I already have the drinks in the fridge at home, chilling. Girl, I can't believe this though. I can't believe that you are going through this. I knew when you said you were going to go out it would be drama, but I thought it would have been once you got back home. Never would I have imagined any of this. But, real talk Tiff - since we have started to build our friendship again, I have really been worried about you with him. All of the shit that he has taken you through really scares me. It just seems that you are in a dark place and you are stuck. I mean, I don't know. Maybe you love him, and maybe you love being a Stepford wife, but it just scares me the way you two are. I am scared that someone is going to call me one day and you will be hurt."

"Honey, you don't have to be scared for me. You might want to be scared for him because it won't just be me it; will be the both of us. Look, we don't need to discuss this and make our night sad. We just need to enjoy ourselves, get dressed and walk in this party like we own it. You know how we do it, there will be plenty for us to look at."

Hell, he is accusing me of being with someone anyway. I might as well go in here and enjoy myself because I know the storm will be a tornado when I get back home. Hell, at this point I may not even have a home to go back to, with all the shit that has occurred in the last 24 hours. I have already been planning my exit in my mind. I am just waiting for my son to graduate high school and I am out. I am taking my baby and we are gone. I knew getting back with him for the millionth time could result in this.

That's why I had him put the cars and the apartment in his name. No way in hell was I going to ruin my credit again after I had repaired it from all of the other times we split. I mean, how many times can a person f--- their credit up and file for bankruptcy? I can't keep doing that. It will cause me havoc at my job, like I said before. I have to pay for my kid to go to military academy because clearly, he isn't going to take care of it. My kid had 13 D1 offers, only to turn them down to go to a military academy that I have to pay 12K for. So, I knew that I wouldn't put my signature on another piece of paper for this dude.

My exit strategy includes me buying property, so no way was I going to let this relationship ruin that again. Trying to file for a separation and moving many times cost me more than money in this relationship. This strategy will be the best thing since sliced bread. Yes, you heard me. I know he probably thinks he has me over a barrel, but little does he know I have been thinking about this for some time. I knew, for some reason, we wouldn't be able to be whole again. Taking the car, taking my purse and my clothes - that's a new level or, at least that's what I thought, but he seems to think that's what will keep me in the house to a slave love. He hasn't seen anything yet. All he has done is brought the beast out in me. I have been nothing but good in this marriage, contrary to his belief.

I went out for New Year's Eve because this hasn't been working for some time and there was no need in trying to fake it in church for one night, for him to act like a total jack ass the following day.

I am so glad that I decided to go to the party, even though, when I got home the next morning it was a hell storm. I was able to handle it. The next morning, I had my aunt pick me up, drop me off back at home with my kid and, yes, it was a hell storm. I decided that I wouldn't entertain it and that made him even madder, of course. I went days again without a car, without my purse with my wallet, and without my belongings. I guess with me going out, he had to have some type of punishment for me.

This dude took my car that was in his name, but I paid for it, and my belongings, and hid it for a few weeks. Yes, you heard me. He hid the car and I had to, again, borrow a car for me to get to work and take my kid to school. I know this all sounds like a movie, but all of this shit really happened. This was all real life. This all really happened.

*'I am still saying, 'Wake me up out of this bad f---ing dream!'
Now, am I saying I am perfect? No, but what I am saying is, no
human deserves this shit. WAKE ME THE F--- UP and shake me*

now!!! All these years of this mental and physical abuse... I just can't do this. This shit is unreal.'

Five minutes of peace in this house feels like months of peace. I'm so glad that he isn't home, because I wouldn't be able to relax while hearing him mouth off about what I have or haven't done. I am sitting in the living room relaxing, finally. I don't think anyone would understand that even ten minutes of peace means the world to me. This dude is never quiet, and all I have needed all these months is quiet time - just a little peace; peace for me to gather my thoughts for my exit plan. Every time he walks in the door, I know it's going to be something.

"Tiffany, where are the kids?"

"They are at my aunt's. Why?"

"Good. You think I am stupid, don't you? You think I am crazy. You think I don't know you been with that nigga. I heard he was looking for you. I know you been with him."

"Look, I don't know what you are talking about, but what we are not about to do is this, when I am in here, relaxing. Man, it's always something with you. You are going to lose your mind if you keep accusing me of someone every single minute. You need to go sit down somewhere and relax yourself, because that's what I am doing, getting some peace." So, I thought.

"F--- your peace B---, you f----- him."

"Look dude, get away from me with this foolishness."

He slaps my face so hard that I feel like my jaw is broken.

"What the f---- is your problem?"

My natural reaction is to kick him. Both my legs go up, kicking him and he falls against the wall. All I can do is grab my jaw and think, 'What the f--- will I tell my kids?' My jaw is broke. Why do I keep dealing with this??

Something is not only wrong with him. Something is wrong with me. I get up, off the couch. He grabs me and locks me in the bathroom. All I can think about at this point is, someone is going to die. My kids are going to come in here and find me dead.

I have to think quick, and I mean quick. This dude just smacked the shit out of me. I know my jaw is broke. My Mom and Dad will kill him. This is about to get ugly; I just see it. I don't even know what dude he is accusing me of at this point. All I know is that I am locked in this bathroom I have to make him feel like it's about him and that I love him. I mean, I thought I loved him, but this shit here isn't love. This is Mr. and Mrs. Smith.

Finally, after about 2 hours of crying and convincing him, he lets me out of the bathroom. All I can think when I look at my face is, 'What in the world?' This is about to get worse. I see it. I feel it. But I am thinking on the bright side at this moment, and still planning my exit strategy. My son graduates high school next month, and then I am planning a vacation to the Essence Festival with my girlfriends, so, this too shall pass, and that I know. Meanwhile, I am icing the side of my face so when I pick my son up in the morning it won't be red and swollen.

"Next month I am going to New Orleans with my girlfriends. Can you keep baby boy for the weekend? If not, I can get Mom to watch him."

"Wait, where did you get money from to go to the Essence Festival? That's a lot that you are spending and taking that from the house to go and party with your friends."

"First off, I am not taking anything from the house when I am the head of the household. I can't remember the last time you paid a bill in here, or have given me any money towards anything, and I haven't said a word. If you don't want to keep your own child, that's fine, but I am gone from July 2nd through to the 6th, so you can let me know, or he will be with my Mom."

Shattered

ssence Festival will never be the same. What happens in New Orleans, stays in New Orleans. Not only did I shut it down, it shut me down. Now, back to reality, and back to what I have to look forward to in this next chapter. My eldest has finished high school and he is off to Military Academy. I am now looking forward to executing my exit plan. I have done this far too long. I am not even sure when the lease is up, but I am more than sure I will be out of here before it is, and so thankful that my name is not on it, so I will not have to worry about the repercussions of leaving. I have done more than enough taking care of this house, for long enough.

Between the two of us we have dealt with quite a bit. I never once was caught cheating, contrary to his belief that there is another man, or many men, for that matter. However, during the many separations, I have not only caught him in the act with other women, but he was living with another woman. When I found that out, what did I do? Still take him back because I believed that, that's what GOD wanted - He wanted me to work it out. However, me figuring my exit strategy out showed me different though, because even though I forgave him and allowed us to do this many times, he would still go back to the other woman I caught him with. He seemed to also blame me for that, because he assumed that I didn't want him, or I wasn't doing my part. How could he possibly think that when I was the one with the sex addiction? I gave him all the sex I thought he needed. I guess he was also trying to come up with his exit plan, but it backfired on him. I never blamed the other woman, nor did I care about her, because he had to be held accountable for his actions. It was a weak excuse as to why he did it. I don't even think I had the time to think about ever trusting him again. I just knew that after that, that was the last straw and I had to act fast on my exit strategy.

"Tiffany, who is this dude texting you at 8 am. talking about good morning?"

"Why are you in my phone? I don't know who it is. What did it say? Whatever the name says, that's who it is."

"Did you meet this dude in New Orleans?"

"I did. I met a few men in New Orleans, so whatever the name says, that's who it is."

"Why the f--- are you giving out your number for niggas to be calling you. I told you!! I knew you were cheating on me, all this time!"

"Dude, you have to be kidding me, if you think I have been cheating on you. If that's what you want to think because someone sent me a good morning text, then you were supposed to see that. If that's what's going to make you change your behavior then, hey, it is what it is. Why would you be in my phone anyway?"

"You left it on the bathroom counter so you must want me to see it."

"I have nothing to hide but it's my phone, and who's calling me really isn't any of your business. You clearly had shit going on that I wasn't aware of, nor did I care. But again, if you must know, it's someone that I met with no intentions of anything other than being friends."

"You lying B----, you had me watch my kid while you went out of town with your whoring-ass girlfriends."

"Look dude, I told you I don't know who you think you keep talking to, calling me out of my name. I have had enough."

"You heard me B---, you lying f---ing c---. You out here in the streets giving up my body to these niggas. This is what you want? You really think you ready for this? I will kill you and these niggas."

"Dude, you have lost your mind? I am not dealing with this today, or any other day. I am getting my kid. We are out."

"You are not f---ing going anywhere. Sit your ass down."

"Who do you think you are talking to? I am not your child."

"B----, you are going to tell me who this is and where the f--- he lives at."

"I am not telling you anything, and what you are going to do is, get out of my way. I am not sitting in here listening to this or have you talk to me like this. You have called me every name but what my name is for years. You probably don't even know what my name is anymore, do you?"

"F--- you B----, you are a f---ing whore!"

"Dude, get out of my way! If you don't get out of my way you will leave me no choice but to call the police."

"You are not f---ing calling anyone!"

"Who the f--- you think you talking to?"

"You are my wife! I do what the f--- I want to you!"

"Oh, you think so! I don't think so!"

Again, I now have to play the mind game of calming him down and making him think that I love him so much, and it's only him because, honestly, I don't know what's going to happen next. I know once I get him to calm down, I am out the door with my kid. This weekend I will rent a U-Haul and I will take all of my stuff to storage if I don't find me a place before the weekend.

Yes, you heard right, for the millionth time, I am walking away, and this time will be the last time, I can promise you that. No way in hell will I do this again. I know I have said this many times, but I honestly don't know how much more my mental state can take of this. I am more than sure anything worse than what's already occurred will put me somewhere in a straight jacket. My girlfriends are worried. My family members are worried. I can see it in them. One of my girlfriends always says how worried she is. It's no need to be worried. I just have to follow through on my plan. That's the goal - to execute the exit plan. And this time, when I do, to make it a final one. I am going to leave here today, stay at my aunt's house tonight with my boy so that we can have peace, and then I will return tomorrow while he is at work. How much does this dude think a young kid can stand to watch happen? The first thing he will say is, 'He is ok, shit happens. He needs to see this.' Dude, no, he doesn't. This will ruin him. No two grown adults should be this dysfunctional in front of their children. I can't even begin to say or recap all the stuff this baby has endured between the two of us, and now this?- A huge blow-up because you see a guy's number in my phone. I have had enough. Like I have said before, with all of the folk that I have been accused of, you would have thought I actually made good on one of them. This is your issue, not mine, and you have to figure this out. I am not staying here tonight.

"Mom, wait, I don't feel comfortable going in the house yet."

"What you mean son, you don't feel comfortable going in? It's fine. I don't think that he is here. I don't see his truck. We can go in, get our stuff, and go back over to our aunt's. We don't have to stay here."

"No Mom. No, let's just not go in. I don't feel comfortable with going in. He may try to fight you."

"Ok son, just because you don't feel comfortable, I will take you back over to auntie's, and then I will come back to get the rest of our clothes. Then, this weekend, I will come and move the rest of our belongings out of the house. I am so sorry Son, that I have to have you involved in this. Let's go. I will take you over to auntie's, and then I will come back after I drop you off."

"Mom, please be safe. I don't want you to come back but I know you have to. I just don't feel comfortable and I don't trust what may happen."

"Son, all you have to do is pray everything will be ok. I have to get clothes for us. We can't wear the same clothes. So, I am going to drop you off, and then I will be right back to get you. I promise. I will be right back to be with you once I get our stuff."

I walk up to my door once again, only to notice that the locks have been changed. You have got to be kidding me" This motherf---er has changed the locks on me again.

Breathe. I can't believe this. I stay out one night, and the locks are changed. This dude really changed the locks. He really thinks that this is going to change what's happening. Changed the locks? This really isn't happening! Did I just go to my door and I can't get in. He had the locks changed!

"Excuse me Sir, do you have a screwdriver?"

"I am sorry Ma'am, what do you need a screwdriver for? Are you trying to get into the apartment upstairs?"

"Yes, I am. I live there."

"Oh, I am sorry Ma'am. He instructed me not to let you in, or for you to get the key."

"WHAT? What the f--- you mean? I live here."

"Ma'am, you are not on the lease and I can't give you the key. I am sorry. I am sorry, I don't know what's going on, but I can't lose my job."

"Thank you Sir, I am sorry I even asked."

"Come now Torrie, come now. I hear all these sirens. I don't know what's going on, but I see all of these police coming up the hill. I don't think they are for me but, come please."

"Ok, I am on my way Tiff. Are you ok? Yes, I am ok now, but I just need you to get here quick."

"Excuse me Ma'am, come here. Where is your weapon?"

"Are you talking to me officer?"

Yes Ma'am. Come over here. Where is your weapon?"

"Officer, I don't have a weapon."

"Ma'am, get over here, put your hands up. Let me see your hands."

"Officer, I am sorry, I think you have the wrong person I live in this building and I was just trying to get in my apartment."

"Ma'am, someone reported that you were attempting to break in an apartment. Please put your hands behind your back."

"Officer, put my hands behind my back? I didn't do anything."

"Ma'am, are you going to listen, or do I need to force you?"

"Ok officer, but I am just asking what's going on."

"Ma'am, do you have your ID?"

"Yes Officer. As you can see, my address is here on my ID."

"Ma'am, well it was reported that you were attempting to break in."

"Officer, I think I can explain after you finish frisking me. If you would allow me to take my hands from behind my back and allow me to be normal, I can explain. I don't have a weapon and I didn't have a weapon. Officer, I have been arguing with my spouse and he changed the locks. I asked the maintenance man if he had a screwdriver so that I would get in my garage. I am so confused right now Officer. You had me put my hands behind my back, accuse me of a weapon without even asking me first."

"Ma'am, I am following protocol."

"What is protocol? You just assuming that I had a weapon? Officer, you seen me walking up the street, swinging keys.

Officer, can I just get you to allow me into my home and get some belongings out?"

Meanwhile my spouse is sitting in the car, watching the officers speed up the street with the sirens, and watching him have me cuffed and questioned without saying one word. Talk about ready to chop his head off. I was like, 'This has to be a bad dream, and no one is willing to wake me up out of it.' Somehow, at this point, I just felt like everyone wanted me to suffer. Everyone. It's no way that my spouse, from who I have put up with so much shit, would call the police, lie and say that I was breaking into my own home, then sit and watch the police cuff me, question me, and then give me five minutes to get my belongings out of my home that I paid the rent on. Yes, you heard that right, five minutes to get my belongings.

"Auntie, come now, come now!"

"What do you mean? Are you ok? I am on my way."

"I have five minutes to get my belongings out of the house. He called the police on me. I am standing here with the police, and because my name isn't on the lease, they are giving me five minutes to get what I can out of the house."

"WHAT?! I am on my way!"

Finally, my aunt arrives and sees police standing all around like I really tried to break in a home that didn't belong to me. As we approach the apartment, I am livid. I am cussing this dude out, calling him everything but his name. You have got to be kidding me! I stay out one night and come back later, and then the next day I'm accused of breaking in. Yes, I call him everything but his name. All of these police are around, standing with their hands on their piece like I am the real criminal.

"Ma'am, are you ready to go in? We can't stand here forever for you to go in. You have five minutes to get what belongs to you. If it doesn't belong to you, Ma'am, you can't take it."

I walk into an empty apartment with two baskets of clothes and my dog.

"WHAT THE F--- IS THIS? Where is my stuff?"

"What stuff Ma'am? This apartment is empty."

I can't f---ing believe my eyes.

"Ma'am, you can work this out later in court, but we can't stand here to try and figure out where your stuff is. This matter will have to be handled with the courts. Our job is to assist at this moment."

"I am filing for a divorce! I HATE you, motherf---er!!! I mean it this time!!! This is it! No way in hell will you ever see me again! No way in hell will I ever be with you again! You have put your hands on me for the last time! You got rid of all my shit that I worked so hard for. This is it. I HATE you, you f---ing loser. You don't have to ever look for me again. I am divorcing your sorry ass."

"Ma'am, let's go. You have to go, or he will press charges against you."

"F---him Officer, f--- him!!! He has tried to destroy me for the last time. Just let me get my dog. He can have the rest of this shit. There's nothing left. F--- HIM!!!! I am homeless because of this motherf---er. You have taken everything from me and my kids. We are homeless because of you. Motherf---er. I HATE YOU!!!"

The Mistress

2015- *Walks into Wildfire*. Looking good, feeling good. When you look good, you feel good. But I'm burning inside like hell because I am going through a fire in my marriage. *Touches up lipstick* (Ruby Woo) (*Sprays* Flower Bomb)

"Good evening Mr. Richmond. So glad to finally connect with you. How's your family?"

"Ha! My family is good. How about yours?"

"My boys are good."

"Your boys? Aren't you married?"

"Well, that's a complicated situation."

"I think we all have a complicated situation."

"What do you mean? Aren't you happily married? Well, that's what I was told anyway, when I first met you."

"Ha! And who told you that? Who would know me that well to say I was happily married?"

"Well, aren't all you married men happy? Or at least, that's what you all portray."

"If I was that happy, would I be out having dinner with you?"

"Of course, you would. You are interested in the curiosity that you say you have been chasing for years. We both know men love to have their cake and eat it too."

"What would you like to drink?"

"I will have a Cîroc and pineapple."

"Tiffany, I have been after you for years, but you never gave me the opportunity because you were with your son's father."

"Is that so? Or was it just because you bumped into me at the event and it sparked your interest all over again."

"Sir, I will have a Cîroc and pineapple and a vodka and cranberry please. So, what's so complicated about your marriage, Tiffany?"

"Does it matter I don't want to discuss it? Not something I would bring you into. So, speaking of marriage, how long have you been married? And do you have any kids?"

"I have been married for ten years now but can't say I am happy. I have been going through a few things and I found a few things out about my wife I would have never expected."

"Oh, really? What is that supposed to mean? Something you want to talk about?"

"My wife cheated on me."

"WHAT? Are you serious? No way!" *Giggles. This is starting to be too much, and it's only been thirty minutes.*

"Yes, I am dealing with quite a bit."

"So I see, but I have time, I am listening."

"I am not sure if I should share all of this with you. I mean, this is the first time we have seen each other in years, and I don't want to bother you with my issues. Well, not really issues because I have already dealt with it."

"Well, was it bad enough for you to leave her?"

"Leave her? Nah, I can't leave my wife."

"Oh really, so your wife cheated, and it wasn't bad enough for you to leave?"

"Well, I don't know if she slept with him. I just found some things in her phone."

"Honey, if you found pictures in her phone or some other communication, she has pretty much already given it up. So, you are not leaving? Why, are you waiting to catch her again?"

"NO! Hell NO!"

"So, I am assuming it's too much to talk about and the several drinks we have had clearly are not making you tell me what really happened. Thanks for having me for drinks tonight. Hopefully we will catch up soon. And maybe the next time we catch up you will tell me why you are not leaving. Or should I say, not leaving her yet."

"What do you mean, not leaving her yet?"

"Ha!! You will have to wait and see what I mean."

"Tiff, don't do that. Tell me why you said that."

"Have a good night Mr. Richmond. We will catch up soon."

"Are you available on Monday?"

"I am off on Monday and we can meet then, if you're available?"

"Sure, just give me a call."

Galleria Tyson's

"Good evening Mr. Richmond. So glad to see you again."

"What would you like to drink?"

"Interesting we are meeting in a bar again."

"I am staying here at the hotel tonight, so the bar is not intentional."

"I will have water please."

"WATER? Sir, she will have a Cîroc and pineapple."

"Oh, you remembered!"

"Of course, I did. I pay attention to what I am interested in. Tiffany, I wasn't expecting you to show up."

"Why? Why wouldn't I show up? Because you are married? When we last met at Wildfire, you asked me to come meet you again, right? Why wouldn't I? We are starting a friendship, right?"

"Honestly, I wasn't expecting you to follow through."

"Ha! How could I not? Our first encounter was intriguing."

"Oh really, how is that? I mean, you have always turned me on but I guess it was just more now with the last conversation we had".

"Here we go with the 'always wanted you' line. You have only had a conversation with me a few times, and we have only met one time before this. I guess that's your line to try and reel me in, huh?"

"Why wouldn't I? I told you I have been after you for about 20 years, but you were into your son's father. I told you that when I first ran into you."

"Interesting considering I never knew that."

"How would you know that if you were so into him?"

"Don't you think I would have noticed if you were chasing after me? I mean, I seen no signs of you after me. I don't even remember ever seeing you."

"You don't have to remember seeing me. I have told you several times, and the truth repeats itself."

"Would you like to come to my room? It's been a long day and I am a little tired. We can go to my room to finish watching the game and chill."

"Ummmmm, I am not sure about that. You think your wife would like that?"

"I thought we wouldn't discuss our baggage. Isn't that what you said when we last met?"

"I did, but I am sure she wouldn't want other women around her husband just relaxing in his hotel room."

"Ok, ok you're right. I did say that, and I won't. Because what goes on with her isn't any of my business, and what goes on with me with her husband isn't any of her business. I guess I really wouldn't have come here if I wasn't a little interested. And I don't kiss and tell. Oops, did I just say that?"

"What's that supposed to mean?"

"You never have to worry about me letting your wife know anything about us, if you end up being careless. You know, you men don't know how to kiss and not tell."

"Is that so...?"

"Of course. Your behavior will change, and she will recognize it, and, besides, if I do end up giving you a little taste, you will be hooked."

"What makes you think I will be hooked??? Maybe you will end up being hooked."

"Not into getting hooked on what won't belong to me Sir. And you getting hooked will happen because this is like the Nile... And it's very slippery when wet. And the real reason you would get hooked is because I am Madam Good P----"."

"Whoa! Never heard that!"

"And three, I am the instructor when class is in session. Think that's something you ready to get yourself into?"

"If I wasn't, I wouldn't have asked you to come."

"Oh, but I thought that's not why you asked me to come. How quickly the thoughts of a married man change. *Laughs.*

"I mean, you know what I mean. I asked you to come so we can get to know each other."

"Oh, really? You do know we are both grown, and I know what you're thinking, and it's not just to get to know each other. When a woman decides to come to hotel room...."

"What's with that? We are grown and I am not going to attack you. I just want to spend some time with you. We can just chill and watch the game. You look great, by the way."

"Thank you. I try to take care of myself. It's the water I drink, I guess. Because If I let the stress get to me, I wouldn't look great."

"Stress? Are you ok?"

"Yes, I am ok. It's life, and we have already talked about it, the package and the baggage that I carry."

"I don't mind. I will listen, I told you, I want to be here for you even though you have the package."

"I don't think you want to sign up for this, honestly."

"Tiff, I told you that it's ok, and I am interested in it all. I told you that I would be here for you."

"Yeah, I guess we will see. Is that the case if I don't decide to give you any of this good p----? Then that may not be the case."

"It's not about the p----, it's about us getting to know each other and building a relationship."

"But, but, oh never mind, I said I wouldn't mention it."

Yes don't. Let's not spend time talking about the packages, I would rather spend time getting to know you and what you want and what makes you happy."

"Oh, is that so, haven't heard that in a while."

"Why not? You don't think your happiness is important? You don't think I want to know what's going on in your life, how you are feeling, and your career?"

"I guess, in my experience with married men, I don't allow them to get close to me. This isn't my first encounter with married men. I know how it goes. You guys never leave home and you always have extra tickets in your pocket."

"What the hell is that supposed to mean?"

"You are not leaving your wife, right?"

"No, not at least until my daughter graduates high school, but you never know, I may."

"Yeah right, you are not leaving unless she leaves you. So, who's the extra ticket, besides me."

"What extra ticket are you talking about?"

"The other women, besides me."

"No-one, no-one. I told you, I don't have time for anyone else. I work a lot and I have responsibilities. My wife doesn't work, so how would I have any extra time for all of that?"

"The same way you have time for me!!!"

"Is it ok Tiff, If I jump in shower?"

"Sure, go ahead I don't mind. Make sure you get dressed before you come out." *Laughs*

"So, I guess you didn't hear what I said, or you just wanted me to see your body, huh?"

"I am sorry Tiff! I just figured we are grown. I wasn't trying to disrespect you. But you are comfortable laying across the bed."

"Well, my back started hurting, sitting in the stiff chair. Would you like for me to put some lotion on your back?"

"Sure, no one has ever asked that before."

"What do you mean, no one has asked that before?"

"Well, you are .....oh, never mind, we won't go there."

"I enjoy doing this. I don't mind. Drop your towel...".

"Oh, you feel comfortable with me dropping my towel????"

"You want lotion, correct?? Goodness, talk about a man with a horse! Well, damn, Sir!" *Eyes popping out of head*

"What's wrong Tiff? Tiff, you said your back was hurting. Would you like for me to massage you?"

"Would you? Would you like for me to jump in the shower first?"

"Sure. Can I get back in with you?"

"Nooooooooo, you can't."

Jumps out of the shower and comes into the room

'In my mind I'm preparing to either be really hooked and satisfied, or really disappointed because I have encountered the largest penis ever that can't perform. I mean, I did get in the shower for this purpose, right?'

"Come love, come over on the bed. I have warmed the lotion a little."

"Thank you, looking forward to this. Hopefully you won't let me down." *Sly laugh*

"What do you mean, won't let you down? Anyone can give a massage. That's what you are talking about, right?"

"Ahhh yes, what else would I be talking about???"

"Stop it. We are grown."

"This massage feels great .... but you are poking me in the back."

"HA! I can't help that love. I am hung low and thick."

"Clearly! I feel that."

"Turn over love. Let me massage the front. Wow, you are drenched!"

"I told you earlier, this is the Nile honey, and it's very slippery when wet."

"But I haven't even touched it..."

"You didn't have to. Your thing got me excited."

"Tiff, let me taste it."

"WHAT!"

"You heard me. Let me TASTE it!!!"

"But, then what... I don't want you to just taste it. I may want more...."

"Relax love, let me take care of you..".

"But I don't know if this is right."

"If what is right, love?"

"Me laying on my stomach, waiting for you to caress me, with me dripping down my legs."

"It's ok Tiff. If you don't want me to massage you, I won't."

"It's not that I don't want you to massage me. Of course I want that. I just know what happens when I am dripping down my legs and I am very hot and horny."

"Oh really, I make you hot and horny?"

"Well if you didn't, I wouldn't be laying in this bed with a towel, waiting for you to massage me."

"Relax love, I have been wanting to do this for quite some time now."

"Love, that was amazing! I needed all of that."

"You also needed my tongue between your legs. That was quite juicy I wouldn't have imagined that your juices would have been flowing off my face like that."

"I have to go... What time is it? I have to go."

"What do you mean, you have to go? Did I do anything to hurt you? It wasn't my intention Tiff. Are you ok?"

"Yes, yes, I am ok. I just have to go. I will call you later."

"Tiff, let me walk you out."

"No, I am fine. You don't have to walk me out. I am a big girl."

"What does that have to do with anything? And I am a man."

"Thanks Mr. Richmond. We will catch up soon."

****

"Hello…"

"Hey Tiff, are you ok?"

"Hey Mr. Richmond, how are you? I am good."

"The question is not, 'are you good'. I am asking if you are ok. You left out of the room the other night fast, as if I hurt you. It was never my intention to hurt you Tiff. I just wanted to make you feel good. I am really feeling you."

"Ha! You keep saying you are feeling me, but I haven't even really given you reasons to feel me."

"I am just trying to see where this is coming from. Tiff, why are you trying to figure out something that I am trying to show you? Why don't you just let your guard down and let me show you. I want to be with you."

"Is that so? How do you want to be with me, but you are married, and you are not leaving your wife? I am confused. How does that work? Oh wait, I get it. I am just supposed to see how this plays out and play the role. You do realize that I am married also, right?"

"I do, but you also told me you were going through some things with your package."

"And I also told you my intention is to get a divorce, and I have already started my process. You haven't Sir, and you surely made it clear you aren't leaving. Hey, we will catch up."

"Wait Tiff, wait. When can I see you again?"

"We will catch up; I have to go."

"Why is it you always have to rush off?"

"Look, I have a lot going on, and I don't know if it's ok for me to get caught up. Like I told you before, I have been in other relationships with married men and they never end up good. I have always been the one to get hurt."

"Tiff, I am not going to hurt you. I told you that before."

"You have said a lot. It's not a matter for me to believe them or not, because it's about actions. You told me already that you are not leaving your wife so why should I allow myself to even get caught up after this one encounter. You do realize you are hung low and thick, and I told you in the beginning, where you may have missed that conversation, that I am addicted to good sex. I have a problem. I am going to be expecting you to sex me every day, multiple times a day, not just when you feel like it."

"Tiff, I will give you whatever. Trust me. Just give me a chance. Whatever you want, I will give to you."

"You do realize that's a pretty big commitment to be giving, considering you are married."

"Tiff, I know what I am up against. I want you. I have told you this many times. You never know what can happen between us. Give me a chance. That's all I am asking, is for you to give me an opportunity to show you how I can take care of you. How I can love you and provide for you."

"But then I am left empty by giving you this opportunity because you are not leaving."

"Does that really matter Tiff, that I am not leaving my wife, as long as I am giving you all that you require?"

"How am I even here listening to you try to convince me that this is right? I will look up and it will be years if I allow this. If I even agree to being in a relationship with you it will be five years before you know it. I have filed for a divorce. You haven't, and you have made it clear to me that you are not leaving. I will be sitting on the side of my bed, waiting for you to come. I will be waiting for texts to come through, or calls that may not even come."

"Tiff, I promise you, I will give you all that you need and require. Just trust me on this. Tiff, please give me this opportunity. I feel like I am begging you and I am ok with it. I have wanted you for so long."

"Listen, I will give you this opportunity, but when it's not giving me what I want and require, I can tell you now, I am out. I know this isn't right, and it was only supposed to be a meeting. How did this turn into 'Tiff I want you'? I am so confused right now."

"Tiff, you don't have to be confused. I want you. It's that simple. Something I have been wanting for years. This isn't something that I just woke up and decided."

"We will talk. I have to go."

"Tiff, you always have to go."

"I am sorry, but I have a lot going on. We will catch up in a few days. I am dealing with my issues right now and I don't think it's fair to put it on you. In the last few days I have had a lot going on between you and my husband. This is a lot to process for one person."

"It's nothing to process when I told you, many times, that I got you. I have nothing to do with you and your husband. I want you and I am here for you."

"Yes, you say that, but how am I able to have access to you when I want it? You are not going to be able to have weekends with me. I am married and I am lonely I don't want to be lonely in another relationship. We can just have good sex when I want it Sir. We don't have to have anything other than you giving me good sex when I want it. That is probably more realistic than anything else."

"NO TIFFANY, stop! I want to be with you."

"Yes, you are saying you want to be with me, but what about if you or I fall in love. Then what? Is it even realistic for you to love me when you are already in love with your wife? I am sorry, but I have to be real with myself, knowing how much this can damage the both of us. You do realize that this could cause us both a great deal of pain, if one, we get caught, and two, if it ends for any other reason. I don't know if, after what I have been going through with my husband, I will be able to handle it."

"Tiff, just give me a chance."

****

"Good evening Mr. Richmond."

"Hey love, I missed you. I thought that you would not give me another chance. Thank you for coming to see me."

"It's a lot to deal with. I am sorry. I know I ran off the last few times but it's hard, being the wife and the other woman. You do realize that?"

"Tiff, I do, I am the husband and the other man. It's really no difference, sweetheart. It appears you may be the other woman, but I am also the other man. We are both in a difficult situation, but I want to be with you, and I am not fighting it Tiff. I missed you. I can't wait to put my tongue inside of you."

"Honestly, I need it. It's been a rough few days."

"I figured. I have been calling you and texting you and you are only responding back with a dry text."

"I need you to make me feel good. It's been too many days in-between. I can't wait to feel it inside. I am only having sex with you, or else I would ask you to strap it up."

"Tiff, we don't need to have these conversations anymore. I haven't been intimate with anyone, including my wife."

"Oh really, so you are not even giving her this good penis? Do you really expect me to believe that? She is the WIFE."

"No, I am not, I am only intimate with you, I told you that. I am having only oral sex with her, and that's it."

"Oh my goodness, that's worse, but hey, if I am willing to be involved, this is something I have to deal with. I am just being selfish; I don't want you sucking or licking anyone but me."

"Hey, it is what it is."

"Whew, that felt great! When will I get more of that?"

"Tiff, it's yours. You can have it whenever you want. I will meet you in the morning.

What time do you have to be at work?"

"I get here at five. You can meet me then, before I go out".

"How is that going to work out? Oh, you think that I am going to sex you at your job."

"Yes, why not? What's wrong with that?"

"You are the one who told me you want it whenever, wherever. Tiff, I am here to please you, to make you happy."

"This is about to be exciting! You mean, you are going to sex me any time of the day, anywhere?"

"Tiff, yes love, if that's what you want, I sure can."

"That makes me happy. Like I told you, if we are going to do this, I require sex every day. I prefer oral sex a couple times in the day."

"I can meet you while you are at work. Love, it's whatever you want. I want to make you happy. I want to please you. This is about making you happy. I know, without you telling me, you have been unhappy for some time and I am here to fix that. I have no problem giving you what you need in all aspects of your life. You call, I am here. You text, I will answer. I know what this relationship requires, and I am going to do my part. I just ask one thing from you Tiff - don't disappear on me."

Pay for Play

"Hello, hey love, I am sorry but I am not able to see you anymore."

"What do you mean, you are not able to see me anymore? What's wrong? What happened?"

"Well, you know I just got back from out of town, and it's a mess here at home."

"What do you mean? You went to Essence Festival, right? Didn't the package know that you went? You told me you were going, so I am pretty sure that you told him. He is your spouse."

"I did tell him. I did. Unfortunately, when I got back all hell broke loose."

"Wait, what do you mean? When we met you told me you weren't involved with anyone else, so what happened? Did he catch you? Did he have your phone records? What's up? Talk to me."

"Well, when I got back, I left my phone in the bathroom and someone I met there, at the Essence Festival, sent me a 'good morning' text and I didn't know how to explain it."

"Wait, what?! You gave your number to a nigga at the festival?"

"Wait, just listen."

"What you mean, just listen…. Now you wonder why he is flicking on you and freaking out? I mean, you did give him a reason to go off. But what does that have to do with you seeing me?"

"Well, he is on my back and we have been arguing for a few days."

"Tiff, but you caused this. Why wouldn't you keep your phone close to you when you knew you were already talking to me."

"Usually I don't leave my phone laying around. I was getting in the shower and then I went to get a towel and I walked out of the bathroom. I left my phone on the counter."

"Tiff, you are slipping, so now I am not going to see you because you gave another nigga attention and added someone into this equation. You are kidding me, right?"

"You are trying to turn this on me, nah that's not what's happening here. I will talk to you later, or whenever."

"Wait Tiff, what do you mean, whenever? What is that supposed to mean?"

"Listen, I am not going to sit here and let you get on me when I am already dealing with my spouse. I will let this pass and then I will give you a call. Take care."

"Tiff. Tiff!" *hangs up phone*

****

"Good Morning Tiff…"

"Good Morning Mr. Richmond, how are you?"

"I am calling to check in on you. I haven't heard from you in a few weeks."

"I told you the last time that I talked to you, things were getting difficult."

"No, what you told me was that you slipped up, which meant you had to fall back altogether because you couldn't keep your home straight."

"What the hell is that supposed to mean? I went out of town with my girlfriends, I didn't go looking to find someone to sleep with or be with. You do know when you go out of town to events as such, you meet other individuals."

"Tiff yes, I do, but you slipped up love."

"What the hell you mean I slipped up? I didn't slip up unless you are speaking of when we were together."

"Tiff, when can I see you? You keep avoiding me. I haven't seen you in weeks. We got together a few times, but I didn't get a chance to get with you like I really wanted to."

"What you mean, like you really wanted to? You are something else. You do you realize we are not in a relationship, right? You do realize that you are married, and I am trying to figure out what's going on with me?"

"Tiff, you don't have to keep telling me that every time we talk. I know what I am and you clearly agreed to get with me knowing that, so we can move past that now. Back to the question at hand -when am I going to see you? I miss you and I want to see you. And besides, I want to stick my tongue where it was before."

"Look, I can't… I don't have a car."

"What do you mean, you don't have a car…?"

"I didn't want to tell you this. But things got worse and my husband took my car."

"What?!Took your car? So, what are you going to do?"

"I don't know. I don't know. Look I have to go."

"Why is it that you have to go every time I try to talk to you, to figure out what's going on?"

"Sir, this is difficult. I don't even know how to talk about it without feeling like I am going to break down or lose my mind."

"Meet me tonight so that we can talk. Can you get a ride to meet me?"

"I can. Let me call my girlfriend to see if she will let me use her car."

"What time can you meet?"

"Let's meet at 7:00 P.M, at the same place that we met before."

"I will see you then."

"Thank you for meeting me. This is all so difficult. I went to New Orleans and came home to a tornado. While I do realize that my spouse and I were having issues before I left, I don't think I realized it was this bad. Mr. Richmond, I am not going to be able to continue seeing you. My home is in disarray and I don't see it getting any better."

"What do you mean Tiff? I don't want to hear this. I didn't say this when we first met. I want this. I want what we were starting."

"How could you want something that's not even real Mr. Richmond?? I don't understand. This is really too much. I thought that this would work, even with just sleeping with you."

"Tiff, you can't throw in the towel with me. We are just getting started."

"You don't understand. My husband is crazy, and this is only going to get worse."

"Tiff, just think about it…"

"What is there to think about? I know you don't want me to keep saying this, but you are not leaving your wife."

"Tiff, you don't know what can happen, so don't keep saying that. We agreed that we would worry about us and not our spouses."

"I have to go. I have someone else's car. I don't have a car and I have to figure this out."

"Tiff, tomorrow, go get you a car."

"What do you mean? I don't have money for a car right now. I told you in the beginning that I had to send my son to military school because he decided that he wasn't going to take a scholarship. I DON'T have it."

"Listen, we don't have to revisit all of what you said you took care of. I understand that. Trust me, I know what it's like for one person to run the finances. You go and get a car tomorrow and I will give you the money."

"You will do what?"

"You go get the car you want, and I will give you the money."

"I don't have the money to pay you back."

"Tiff, I didn't ask you to give me anything. I asked you to go get a car. I need to see you. I want to be with you. I told you in the beginning that I would be here for you."

"Wait, what? You are saying, go apply for the car and you are going to give me money for the down payment?"

"Tiff, go get you a car. I need to see you."

"Good night Mr. Richmond, I will call you tomorrow. Good Night Mr. Richmond."

"Good Morning Love. Thank you for loving me when I am finding it hard to love myself. I am still trying to just wrap my head around all of this mess that I am going through."

"Tiff, I am here. What do you need? I told you to go look for a car and I would take care of it."

"I know, I know. But there is so much going on. I did apply for a loan so that I can get a car."

"Well, now that we have that out the way, how much do you need? What do you need from me?"

"I am not sure yet, I just applied so I am waiting for them to contact me back."

'Gathering my thoughts': GOD wouldn't bring me a married man, and I know this. But why is this man here while I am going through all of this? I just don't understand. GOD

what's happening? I am going through a fire and You send me someone that is married to recuse me? This isn't Your work. I know it can't be. HELP ME!! GOD, Your word clearly states, "Exodus 20:14 You shall not commit adultery," I know this and I am not trying to make excuses for my behavior, for sleeping with or having a relationship with a married man, but why is this man in my life? How is it he is saving me from my hell, or at least, that's what it appears to be? He is stepping in financially as well as serving my sexual needs. Isn't this what every woman wants? I am going back and forth with trying to figure out what I need while I am in this hell. My mind is all over the place. I am in hell in my marriage and I am feeling like someone actually loves and cares about me. But how can a married man care about me? Oh, because he is giving me money. Because he is supplying all my needs and wants? Talk about a confused individual. I don't really know what's going on with me but what I do know is GOD didn't send me someone's husband to love.'

'Tiffany, why are you doing this? You know this isn't right. GOD, forgive me, for I have sinned. I know this isn't right. I know I shouldn't be trying to be involved with this married man. I have done this so many times before and I know what the outcome is. I know that he is never going to be mine. I know that he doesn't love me. I have to focus on getting myself right. I have to focus on You GOD. I have to pray my way out of this hell. I have to focus on getting my own marriage right. I can make this work in my own marriage. I just have to pray. I just have to pray everything will work out. I am in a constant fight with myself and I know this isn't right, but this just feels good. I love the way he makes me feel. I love that he is stimulating me. I just don't know what to do. I am not happy at home. My husband isn't making me happy. I don't know how much longer I will be able to take

the abuse from my husband. I am not in love with my husband anymore and I am falling in love with someone else's husband. Why would GOD send me this man? Tiffany who are you kidding? GOD will not send you someone else's husband. Why is he in my life? What is his purpose? I know I am at my lowest right now. Is this GOD sending me this man to heal me? Who am I kidding? He isn't leaving his wife. He told me this from day one. I just have to pray it will work out. Maybe he will leave his wife. Maybe he will fall in love with me. Maybe we can move in together. This will work out. I just have to believe that it will. I am just going to go with it until it ends. I am not really looking for anything, so I am just going to hang out with him for peace of mind. I will just serve him sexually. I will make him feel good. I will be the freak that he doesn't have at home and have him take care of me financially. I feel like I am in a bad dream. Is this all really happening? I am married, going through hell, and someone who claims they have been after me for years, is willing to give me the world. I am fighting a losing battle in my marriage and I am starting to have the time of my life with someone's husband. Ok, breathe. Let me gather my thoughts, pray, and start over tomorrow. I can't believe that while I am trying to get out of one mess, I am getting myself into someone else's mess. Wake me up when this bad dream is over. No way am I jumping out of one fire into the next. Maybe I am not jumping into another fire. Maybe this is part of healing. I guess I am just in denial. This feels bad and good at the same time. I guess this is self-medication with someone else's husband.'

"Good Morning love. I guess we are going to play this chase game now that you got caught with someone else, huh?"

"Sir, what are you talking about?"

"I have texted you several times, and called you several times, and you haven't responded."

"Sir, I am lost. I am just trying to find my way through this hell."

"Tiff, I don't know how many times I have to tell you that I am here. You have access to me anytime."

"Oh, really? Any time and any day?"

"Yes, my phone line is open to you."

"We will see how long this lasts."

"It's going to last as long as you want it to last, or until you throw in the towel, because I am not going anywhere. Tiff, did you get approved for the car?"

"I did, yes. I am sorry. That is the good news. They want a $4,000 down-payment. It's a 2013 Range Rover."

"Ok, so when are you going to go get it?"

"Whenever you are ready for me to come get the money."

"Come now. Why are you waiting? I am not understanding why you are making this so difficult."

"What is a good time to come?"

"I will be at work until 7:00 A.M."

"I will be there as soon I can get a ride. I will text you when I am on my way."

"Tiff, I want you to know that you can ask me for anything. I have prepared myself to take care of you."

"Wait, this is more than $4,000."

"I know what it is. You may need more."

"I don't know what I did to deserve this help. When I get back on my feet I will give this back."

"Tiff, go get your ride. You don't owe me anything. Call me after you pick it up and we will get together in the morning before I go home."

"Thank you, Sir. I don't think you know what this means to me."

"I do. You don't have to worry about wanting anything when you are with me. I want to see you in the morning."

"Thank you so much."

"Tiff, stop thanking me. I told you I got you. You are no different than my wife. The only difference is, we are not on paper. I have shown you more than enough that it's not about the sex with me. You are the only one that's addicted to sex."

"I know, you have shown me. You helped me with my son's school. You helped me get a place after my husband put me out, and you helped me with this truck. I know you say I don't owe you, but I am just trying to wrap my head around this."

"No, listen, really though Tiff, I don't know if you realize, but you set this standard in the beginning. You told me straight up that you don't sex for free."

"Sir, no I didn't."

"Yes, you did, and because I want you so bad, I don't have a problem with it. You deserve everything. How could I see you out in the street with no home and no ride? You have your little man to take care of, and your eldest boy. I will do what I have to do, and I don't have to keep telling you that. Your birthday is coming up. What do you want?"

"Yikes, I don't even know if I could really ask you for anything. I mean, you are always doing things for me. There's this Louis Vuitton bag that I have been wanting."

"Let me know and we can go get it this week. Tiff, you do remember you said you were 'Madam', don't you?"

"Where is that coming from Sir?"

"The Madam has me hooked."

"Oh, so because you are hooked, this is the only reason you are doing this. You really don't love me?"

"Tiff, stop. Of course I love you, but you know this comes with it. Let's both be clear. You would not be with me if I wasn't giving you any money, and you and I both know that."

"Well Sir, you might be right. Really though, I want you to know that I do appreciate you being a man, taking care of me and your own home, because you don't have to."

"Tiff, I love you, and I will always love you."

Double Life

"Tiff, I want you to know I love you. I have told you many times, but I want to continue to show you."

"Mr. Richmond, you clearly have shown me, but I must ask, do you understand that you are living a double life? Do you understand that you have created yourself a whole, separate responsibility? This is all so wild to me, and seems like a dream, as I have stated so many times to you. Every day I feel like we are both living in a dream, and when we wake up out of this, it could either be bad or good."

"Tiff, I think that you are putting way too much thought into all of this. I think that you should just roll with it. We know that we are in love and we know that we have each other. You are getting a divorce and you have decided that you are going to be with me."

"Wait… Wait a minute Sir, do you even understand what you just said? You want me to be dedicated to you while you are still in a relationship with me and a whole marriage with your wife? We are now going on year two with this. How long do you think I am going to go for this? Until your daughter graduates, and then maybe, just maybe, you might leave your wife. I can't do that. I am sorry. I don't know if I am going to wait that long. I haven't been sexually involved with anyone else, but this is a bit much Sir."

****

"Tiffany, I see your boo thang and his wife are out to dinner today. Wasn't he just with you this morning?"

"Girl, that's why I didn't even want to log on to social media today. I am not going to even entertain that foolishness. Yes, just what I said, foolishness. I knew what it was when I decided to sleep with him in the beginning. You know we know what it is. I understand it though. He told me from the jump he wasn't leaving his wife and he told me why, so am I the fool for staying involved, or is he the fool for paying? I admit I am in love and I am emotionally attached, but I have to let this thing play out. I can't keep sleeping around and jumping from man to man and, besides, I love him and really, he is the one living the double life, not me. I don't have anyone to answer to. You know how it is. You are doing the same thing I am doing, and you have been doing this married man thing for as long as I have. Hell, you call me for advice on how to get him hooked. Girl, we have it bad. We can't do this forever."

"Tiff, who you telling? But hey, at least he loves you and he takes care of you sexually and financially."

"Yes Girl, that might be true but clearly, he is living a double life. He leaves my house and goes back home, then leaves his house and comes to me."

"Tiff, at least he talks to you about what's going on in his life. Hell, my dude will not talk about what's going on in his life. The only way I see what's going on in his life is I see it on social media."

"Girl, you keep saying 'at least this' and 'at least that'. No honey, it's all the same. It's all WRONG. There is no right in dating or sexing a married man. We are both WRONG. Hell, all of us are wrong. This is a vicious cycle that only we can stop."

"Tiff, who are you fooling? If you wanted to stop this, you would have not started it. You have been doing this for years. The only thing that stopped you before was, you were married. But think about it - you have always had a sex addiction and you have always lived a double life, just like the married man."

"You know what Girl, you are right. I know I said that I would not be doing this with him for long, but it's already been two years, very close to three. Girl, we are the crazy ones though. Could you just imagine being the fly on the wall at their house when they walk in after getting freaked out with us? I mean, you know their favorite line is, 'My wife isn't giving me oral sex, my wife won't sex me the way you do'".

"Girl, no, the favorite line is, 'My wife only likes it missionary style'."

"Girl, I freak him out every time he comes over. It's always my goal to turn him out and do something different every time. It just drives me crazy that they don't realize they are truly living a double life. You are with your wife and family on social media and everywhere else, acting as if your home is perfect, and ten minutes later you are answering my text. Where is the real love?"

"Do you think they really love either one of us at this point? Who's losing here? Clearly not him. He is getting the best of both worlds and we are allowing it."

"Tiff, you are trippin' Girl. You love that dude. So, you are telling me you are willing to give up everything that he is doing for you? You are willing to give up your double life? I don't know what girlfriend you think you're talking to, but you are just as guilty as he is. Now, if we are going to be honest here, let's put this out on the table and be all the way honest with ourselves. You are willing to give up this man that has been taking care of you sexually and financially for two years, because he is living a double life? Yea, think on that one. Come to me with a better one Girl. You escaped an abusive relationship that was going nowhere but to hell, and got with someone who is taking care of you. Tiff, I am waiting. No. No, listen, this isn't right like it's not right for you honey. Just like your dude comes over you give him oral sex and he is out. The next time you hear from him, it's him with his wife on social media, or you see him in the club posted up, waiting for the next whisper in the ear, 'Can I come over?.'"

"NO, we can't keep doing this. We are so much better than being the other women."

"Tiff, you are trippin' if you give that dude up. Why would you give him up? You never know Tiff. It's been pretty steady with you two. You don't know, he might just leave his wife."

"Girl, he isn't leaving his wife, and he is never going to be mine. And if he is mine, don't you get it? He will do the same to me. This is the double life that we will never figure out."

"Tiff, listen, even if you get your "Own Man", how will you know he is just yours? You have been doing this married man thing for so long, you just never know."

"Girl, this is why I have to break this cycle. See, you think it's ok because you know what he is doing for me. But think about it, your dude's not doing anything for you. Don't you see? You are in it and you are not getting jack. Why don't you get out? Why don't you find your own man? We are both better than this. We don't need this life. See, we look at it as 'oh well, we don't have to deal with this or that', but in reality, we are on fire inside and we are hurting ourselves. Girl, you really need to throw in the towel. He gives you nothing but a hard time every time you ask for a dollar. He just thinks he is supposed to come over and get head and then roll. No Ma'am, and then you look up on social media and he's professing his love with his wife after he just left your house and you have swallowed all of his babies. Girl, the bottom line with us both is, we can't continue to allow this to go on in our lives. I know I am living a double life because he is married telling his wife one thing, telling me another, and I am married. This isn't what GOD has for me, and I know it."

"Tiff, here you go with the GOD talk, when you know what you are doing. I get it Tiff. I know you want to live right, but you are missing the mark with this one honey. You have been going back and forth with this for too long. It is what it is, and has been for you for a while. The double life. Do you need me to talk you through it? You and your "MAN" are living a double life. The real question you should be asking yourself Tiff, is when are you going to be real with you and walk away from this double life? This is really scary when you think about it. It's like you both are walking around with a mask waiting to fall off. The next question is, what happens if either of you get caught?"

"Girl, he asked me a few weeks ago what if he got caught? Am I ready for him to move in with me?"

"So, what was the answer, since you seem to have this all figured out?"

"The answer is NO. As a matter of fact, I said hell no."

"Wait Tiff, what do you mean, 'No'?".

"Girl, I can't let him move in with me? Did you forget I have my boys? No way, and I am in the process of trying to get a divorce."

"What does your divorce have to do with it? You are living in a home that this man furnished and gave you the money for."

"Girl, get away from me. This is all too much. I am going to tell you what I am going to do. I am going to let him live his double life. And I am going to live my life. I am going to work through my divorce. I am going to let him figure out his lying, deceitful double life and, in the meantime, I am going to let him continue to sex me the way he has. Girl, the real question is, what are you going to do? Clearly, we both have a situation on our hands. Just because you are single and dating married men, doesn't make it any better for you, you do realize, that right? I just don't get it, and maybe I never will. He says he loves me. He acts like he loves me, but he is married. Love is a verb and a noun."

"Tiff, come on now, here we go with this school mess."

"No, really listen. I know you are blowing me off and you don't want to hear this but, how could someone be in love with two women like that? I think its lust, I really do. I think I am just giving him a sexual feeling that he hasn't had."

"Tiff, you have got to be kidding me. Do you even sit back and think about all the things this man has done for you? Hello! Wake the hell up out of your dream Girl. Look Tiff, you just need to figure out, either you're going to live in sin, wait his wife out, or get your life right, period. That's the only advice I have for you right now. I clearly can't judge you because I am calling you for advice on how to keep my married man hooked. So, I am going to say this. Stay in it and wait it out in sin, or get your life right. I will be here for you either way. I am on the no-judging zone."

"Girl, I hear you, but I am going to leave it at this. I think it's all just a part of deceitful lust. He says love because he thinks that will keep me. Living a double life while being deceitful to me and his wife is what it really is."

Deceitful Lust

For three years I have been involved in a relationship with a married man. I am guilty of misleading myself while being involved in my own deceit. While I wanted to believe this was a relationship that GOD brought me, I was only fooling myself. Like, who am I kidding? GOD won't bring you a married man, and He surely won't ruin someone else's marriage to make your life easier. While I assumed this man was brought in my life to heal me, clearly he was brought in my life to make things more difficult.

How could I allow myself to fall in love with someone else's husband? How could I even think it was ok to brag to my girlfriends about being with someone's husband, when they were also married? Did they ever really trust me around their husbands if they knew this? Did I even think about that, or care? No, because I was too selfish, living in my own deceitful lust and engaging with a married man. Nothing else mattered. So, I am telling my girlfriends about this relationship, not even realizing that they probably really didn't trust me around their husbands, but they would never admit that, of course. The only thing that mattered was I was being financially taken care of, as well as sexually taken care of, and I had no worries of no longer being financially stable. I was now having a somewhat stable mind, and most of all, I was being sexually satisfied every day, several times a day.

What more could someone, who has been through hell in their own marriage, really want and desire at this point? Lust and love, right? Isn't that what we are all looking to get after being in a relationship that brought nothing but pain? After all the hell I went through, I know I had only decided that whatever was going to be next had to be good. It didn't matter if he was married or not. I have been doing married men before I was married. I knew being involved with married men really meant no real commitment, and I was free to be me. But what I didn't face was that he would truly never leave his wife, no matter how much he proclaimed to love me, or wanted to be with me.

This was all a part of the deceit in the relationship. In being with this married man for so many years, I did whatever he asked or desired to satisfy all of his sexual needs that he claimed he wasn't getting at home. Hell, to me it didn't even matter if he was or wasn't getting at home. I was addicted to sex and all I know is, I wanted to be sexually satisfied, no matter the consequences or the cost. We were so engaged in lust that, so many times he would ask me to come to his home while his wife was out of town. That is the only time that I drew the line in the relationship. I recall telling my sister that I had considered going to his home to sex him all over his house. I recall my sister saying, "Make sure I have your insurance information, because if the wife comes home, she is going to kill you and him."

I instantly had to check myself. But at the time that he asked, I didn't even think about it. Nothing mattered but making him happy and me being sexually satisfied.

This is what DECEITFUL LUST looks like. You will do anything. It doesn't matter whose feelings are involved, and it doesn't matter about the circumstances. You are just all in for your own selfish reasons. This is what a sex addiction looks like - 'I have to have it. I want it and nothing is going to stand in the way of me being sexually aroused. He asked me to come to his house and I am going and will deal with it later'.

Thank GOD for sisters, I can honestly say she may have saved my life. When you are in a relationship with a married man, either you are all in, or you are not. I was all in, whatever it took, whatever he wanted and whatever I wanted. This seemed like the perfect relationship, except he was still married, and I was waiting for my divorce to go through. All of the things that I was doing right and all of the things the wife was doing wrong. The wife isn't sexing him and, if she is, it's not how he enjoys it anymore. I was the freak wearing the heels, the lipstick and the lingerie. The one standing on my head, doing backflips for him. The one giving him the dynamic head that he longs for each day when he gets off, or while he is driving down the highway. He races to see me because I am not nagging him about anything when he gets off. I am the one he can 'pillow talk' with, and it's not going to go anywhere because I am the mistress.

This is not love. This is all lust. There is a difference between the two. These are all lustful desires that these men crave for whatever reason. It's something different than what they are getting at home. The wife surely isn't driving down the highway having him pull his penis out. The wife isn't pulling over on the side of the road and allowing her man to give her oral sex. Who are we kidding? It's a lustful desire that these men are craving and it's women like me that are addicted to this behavior, and this is how I have engaged for so many years of being the mistress. LUST takes over and becomes a part of a deceitful behavior that I accepted. We accept this behavior as the mistress because we try to convince ourselves, 'if the wife isn't taking care of his needs, I will'. It's a falsehood that he will leave his wife one day and eventually turn the hoe into the housewife.

Honey, he isn't leaving. I don't care what you try to do. At some point in all of these years of being with this man, I fell in love and hell, maybe he did to. But what I do know is I was EMPTY every time he left me. No matter how many hours he sexed me, how much money he gave me, he left me with an empty feeling as the years started to pass by. I eventually started to question myself. Was the money worth it any longer? Am I missing out on a single man that could potentially do the same things for me that this married man was doing? I had to shake this emptiness off somehow. But how was I going to do it when, after every sex session, the money was getting longer but the time in between the sex sessions was also getting longer. Was he giving me more money because now, either his wife is on to him, or it was someone else involved? I had to figure out what I would do to combat the emptiness.

Emptiness

H ow many times are you willing to be left empty before you are dead? Yes, dead internally. Do you really enjoy waiting for the next text? Waiting for the next visit? Waiting for the next call? Is it really worth sitting for days, maybe even sometimes for a week, before you have the next sexual encounter? Are you willing to sacrifice your soul to someone that doesn't belong to you, but to another woman?

The lust, the lies and the emptiness that you feel after you have just allowed your soul to connect to someone else. Sitting on the side of the bed after he is long gone and back to his wife, not knowing when he would return again, is emptiness. Waiting days for the next encounter is emptiness. Chances are you walking around mad at the world because you don't know when you will have another encounter with the man you poured your soul out to. Yes Sis, I said it right, someone that you would like to be your man. You are waiting for the next lie that he will be over, and he won't show. You have just poured out your soul in your last sexual encounter with this man. Each and every time that you exchange your soul with him, he is getting filled and you are getting empty.

Don't be fooled that he loves you or he cares. HE DOESN'T. How could he? Do you really believe that he does? If he did, you wouldn't have emptiness when he leaves. You wouldn't wonder when is the next time you will see him. You do realize that there is never a real commitment to hook up for the next time. When you ask, 'When will I see you again?', you already know what the answer will be. 'I will call you and let you know, because I have to see what I have going on.' Sis, if a man loves you and wants to be with you, he won't have to see what's going on, because he will always be available to you. He won't have to validate his schedule with his wife, or anyone else for that matter. He won't have to decide to see you. After each encounter you have with him, you are only happy for seconds. After realizing that you don't know when the next time will be, you are immediately left with feeling empty. This empty feeling is due to the fact you have poured out all of you and haven't received anything back. You continuously pour out and nothing is poured back into you. The more you pour out will be the less you have for each encounter, until there is nothing left.

Sis, at this point you are empty. You have allowed a married man to drain you of all you have because he can never make you full. You will never have happiness or joy in being the mistress. Ask me how I know. I was a professional mistress for years until the emptiness had my body on fire.

Yes, you heard me.

The emptiness eventually had my soul on fire. After each encounter I would start to have the craziest feelings. I would start to question myself. Why do I accept this? Why do I think it's ok to accept this? What am I getting out of this? All of these thoughts would run through my mind while I am left sitting on the side of the bed, or in the car, after he is long gone. Long after the sexual encounters and the money being spent, I am alone, waiting for the next encounter. How do you honestly think you can be whole, if all you are doing is pouring out with nothing being poured back into you. When we pour out we need to be naturally poured back into. Our souls are crying out for love, connection and commitment. We will start to fill these feelings with lust, lies and other addictive behaviors, because we are empty and want to be filled.

At what point to do you decide that you will no longer give yourself to someone else's man? I know I have said this many times, and I will continue to say it. He won't leave his wife or his family. If his wife doesn't decide to divorce him, he will stay. He will continue to empty your soul while he is pouring into himself. No, I am not bashing him, because you are allowing it to happen. You have to decide that you don't want to be empty. You have to decide that you won't sit on the side of the bed in a towel, alone, after you just had the best sexual encounter, or so you thought. Your hands are on your forehead and water is dripping down your body. He didn't even have time to dry you off.

Isn't that enough for you to change this behavior? It was enough for me. Way too many times after the best sexual encounter, and the best shower experience, I was left with water dripping off my body with him already gone. Yes, you read it right. He was already gone before I was even dry. This feeling always left me with complete absence of Satisfaction, even after I thought we just had the best sexual encounter. I always thought that our sexual encounters were the best, each and every one was amazing. I kept trying to convince myself that this was the best sex I have ever had. I was blown away with the oral sex.

It was after the last shower encounter that I knew it was an emptiness that I no longer wanted to feel. When the water drips were still falling off of my body and he didn't even stay long enough to dry me off, I knew I had to disconnect from the adulterous behavior that left me empty for the last time. I was experiencing emptiness that had me plunged into an inner abyss that resulted in me having an additive and escapist behavior of a sexual addiction that I couldn't control.

Don't let this be you, and if it is, save yourself. You still have a chance to get out, just like I did. You don't have to live in this empty feeling. You can change the dynamics and disconnect from the adulterous behavior. Start loving yourself from the inside out. Start receiving the unspeakable joy of loving yourself. Free yourself from the chains that's you have been locked into for so long. He doesn't love you, nor does he respect you enough, leaving you to live this empty life. Pour back into yourself and be filled with the love of 'You', honey. You no longer have to fill his needs. You can start to fill your own needs.

You are not only left alone after the sexual encounters. You are also left alone on holidays. It's Christmas and you won't even receive a text because he is tied up in his family. It's your birthday, and your birthday dinner, and you are either alone or with your girlfriends. Its Thanksgiving and you damn sure are not breaking bread with him and his family. You might get a text, but it won't be on the holiday; it will be after the holiday.

Don't you deserve more than this? Aren't you worthy of more? If this behavior doesn't show you it's time to disconnect, then I'm not quite sure you will ever learn to love yourself. Love yourself enough to pour back into You what was left empty by a man who can never fill you up. You have to learn how to survive in the hell you created when you decided to engage in adulterous behavior.

You can survive without this behavior.

You can survive without being empty.

You are ENOUGH.

"Your body is a temple of the Holy Spirit who is in you, whom you have from GOD". 1 Corinthians 6:19

Surviving in Your Hell

I had the inside of my body feel like a fire for quite some time. I would often have a burning sensation inside my calf for months. I could never figure this out. I would literally be standing, and my leg would be on fire. I often used to think to myself this was GOD speaking to me. This was my opportunity to get it right. This was my opportunity to change my life. Something could be going on with my health because I wouldn't surrender completely to GOD. I was playing with fire. I always blew off the fact that GOD could be potentially punishing me for being an adulterous woman. There was a burning feeling way too often. I was burning, literally, inside of my body. My girlfriend always asks me why wouldn't I ask GOD to deliver me from this adulterous behavior? If I had asked GOD to deliver me, I knew that he would. I wasn't ready to stop playing in the devil's den and I was being disciplined by GOD, and I knew it.

For three years my marriage was a total disaster. While my marriage was in a total disaster, I engaged in an adulterous relationship for another three years. In deciding to engage in an adulterous relationship I thought it would be healing, because it just felt right in the beginning. How could I get with a man who would turn my world around after being in a disastrous marriage? Looking back, I know it wasn't GOD. But what I do know is, I survived in my hell. I went from a failed marriage to a survival adulterous relationship. I wanted to be healed in all the wrong places. I wanted someone else's husband to heal me. No way was that really ever possible. I went from a full-time relationship to a part-time lustful deceitful relationship. Neither was healthy for me and GOD tried to save me many times, but I was defiant and in denial. I wouldn't listen to GOD. I wanted the sexual demon. I wanted it and I thought only this married man could give me what I needed. He was taking care of my sexual needs and my financial needs. I was no longer living in an abusive relationship and I thought this is what life was about. I thought I was actually surviving in my hell. I had finally decided to file the paperwork for my divorce and pray that he would eventually leave his wife. I was living in denial, while surviving in my hell. I thought all my needs were met. While I was surviving in my hell, I was praying that my mental stability would stay intact. It was three years of hell, followed by three years of confusion. I wanted to be loved. Let's face it, doesn't every woman want to be loved by a man? Or, at least, that's what we portray. But how can we truly be loved by a man when we don't love ourselves? We can't expect a man to love us if we can't show him how we love and respect ourselves.

For over a year I felt the emptiness, I felt that there was no burning desire that he wanted to be with me and only me anymore. There were signs to me that maybe he had even started to be with another woman, other than me and his wife, or he possibly started to fall back in love with his wife.

It was an empty feeling followed by a burning feeling, that I had to start thinking of my exit plan. Yes, you heard me. I am now not only filing for a divorce, but I am thinking of an exit plan from my adulterous behavior. This is quite a bit to be dealing with, all while trying to keep my mental stability and raise my children, while working a full-time job. Looking back, GOD loved me so much that I didn't end up in other addictive behaviors with all the hell I was in. The only thing I can tell you is, GOD loved me more than I loved myself.

Romans 5:8 "but GOD shows his love for us in that while we were still sinners, Christ died for us."

Ephesians 2:4-5 "But GOD, being rich in mercy, because of the great love with which he loved us, even when we were dead in our trespasses, made us alive together with Christ - by grace you have been saved."

Sacred or Street

Waking up each day, trying to decide if you will allow the devil to use you, or will you allow GOD to take control, is an everyday battle. While it may not seem as such when you are dancing in the lion's den, it truly becomes a task trying to beat your addiction, no matter what the addiction is.

For me it was an everyday battle trying to beat my sex addiction. I wanted it every day, two or three times a day, and this man was supplying my sexual addiction needs. There was no love, there was only lust. I knew what was at stake with us being together, so why would I go back and forth with trying to decide to live right and get closer to GOD, or continue with this deceitful, lustful behavior? Neither one of us, at this point, was winning. At this point, I was going to church, trying to build my relationship with GOD, while leaving church to be filled with sinful behavior. How could I win doing this? There was nothing to gain, leaving church, being filled with the Word of GOD and then meeting a married man. This has to come to an end. I am praising GOD while engaging in sinful behavior. I was in denial and most importantly, I was confused and again, my mental stability was being challenged. Why would I keep creating this self-inflicted pain? I was smart enough to know that GOD would not bless my mess, nor would there be any blessings out of me bouncing back and forth with being an adulteress. GOD's Word is true.

1 Corinthians 6:18 'Flee from sexual immorality. All other sins a person commits are outside the body, but whoever sins sexually, sins against their own body".

This was against my own body. How could I not care about my own body? How could I keep taking a risk with my body? I knew it could be a chance that I could possibly get a sexually transmitted disease. How could GOD keep letting me escape this madness? Thank GOD that I didn't get any sexually transmitted diseases. I knew he was sleeping with his wife and there was a small possibility that he could also have been sexually involved with someone else. I had to pick a side and Ma'am, you also need to pick a side. You won't always be lucky to escape the risk.

GOD's Word doesn't change, and as many times as I have stayed with the Word of GOD, I defied it, thinking it would be ok. It never was ok. I was dancing with the devil and I knew it. In order for GOD to turn my life around I had to pick a side. I had to decide what side I would be on. Would I be on the sacred side, or would I be on the street side? Yes, you may be wondering why I would have to pick a side, but when you have any kind of addiction, you have to pick a side if you want to be delivered. There are no 'both sides', and there definitely isn't 'I want to go back and forth when it works for me for that moment'. What if his wife caught us? What if we got caught while engaging at his job? What if we got caught while engaging all the wild places that we were at in the heat of the moment?

Choosing to be sacred and change your life, or run the streets to destroy your life, literally.

Living in your own world without wanting to have consequences just isn't realistic. Addictions, no matter what, come with real consequences. This addiction was very demonic, just as many other addictions are, and they are very real and very hard to beat. The only way to beat your addiction is to surrender and submit to GOD and decide that you will give it all up to be pure and sacred. GOD saved me from myself. Self-inflicted self-destruction almost destroyed me. Yes, I know you will say it was just sex. It was more than sex. It was an addiction that I let take over my life. I was walking around like everything was ok but honestly, it wasn't. I had to decide and decide fast to put fire in my faith and let go. Let go of what didn't belong to me, someone else's husband. I was ready to activate my faith and become the sacred woman that GOD created me to be. I decided that I didn't want this anymore. I wanted to walk out on faith. I wanted to let GOD handle this. It was starting to get to overwhelming for me. I was ready to be delivered. I was ready to stop abusing my body and mind. I decided that I would no longer have limits on my life. I was ready to heal. I was ready to add the fuel to my faith. I am giving up the street. I am giving up being the MISTRESS. I no longer wanted this life. The fire in my faith will save me from my own burning desires of allowing this addiction to control my life.

Fire in My Faith

E very day that I awake, I am fighting my sexual addiction, but GOD told me that I can be free. Every day the chains that the devil had around me, are falling off of me. While most of my deceitful, lustful behavior was self-inflicted, I allowed the devil to control my mind, body and soul. I always trusted GOD but I never had a relationship with GOD. I always wanted GOD to save me. I just never submitted or surrendered to GOD. While my sex addiction controlled me, and the financial addiction controlled me, it wasn't until I was at my lowest that I knew I had to submit and surrender and completely let go and 'Let GOD', literally.

In all of my hell, and in all of my distress, I didn't have time to go for a therapy session with a therapist. While that may work for some, it wasn't a choice for me. I didn't have a lot of time to try to figure out the next move. The only option I had was to surrender and submit and let GOD. We all have situations that can literally make or break us, and what you decide, will be. Every day I had two boys watching me, so there was no 'quit' in me. They had both already seen enough so I couldn't let them down anymore. They didn't choose me, I chose them, and they damn sure didn't ask for this life that I dealt to them. It was time for me to put my faith in action. My faith needed the fire to be ignited and allow GOD to use me. GOD literally saved me from myself. I was at the point of no return of self-destruction. I was tired of living a lie, always pretending that I was ok, when I was on fire inside. Fighting my faith, fighting what I knew was right.

My mental stability was being challenged more than I wanted it to, and my body had been used for sexual gratification for not only me, but others. Hell, I was lucky to make it out with a clean body after all of the encounters that I had. At this point, realizing all that GOD had already saved me from, it was time. Waking up every day, deciding that I was either going to keep letting the devil use me or allow GOD to take control. It was time for me to put fire in my faith and allow GOD to use me. It was time to walk out in faith and know that no matter what was ahead of me, I would no longer be held captive to sex and money and greed.

So many times, as I have said before, my girlfriend would always ask me why I would not pray myself out of this situation. She had seen me pray and stay the course when I was in distress in my marriage/ Why couldn't I do the same for the adulterous relationship? One day I woke up and decided that I had to pray, I had to pray and pray some more. I had to be free. I had to step out in faith and know that GOD would take care of me completely. Although this man had provided for me financially, it was time to cut the cord and depend on GOD completely. I had all the reasons to do so. At this point I was empty; my body was on fire and I truly had no reason to stay, as I knew he wasn't leaving his wife. All of the reasons for me to stay were stacked up against me and it was time to fold with this adulterous relationship. As GOD's word states:

Hebrews 11:1 'Now faith is the substance of things hoped for, the evidence of things not seen'.

This is what I had to do. It was no longer a option. I decided that I would allow GOD to take over and go out in faith. I decided that I would not go back and forth with 'what if it didn't work'. I decided that I would finally pray myself out of this relationship. As crazy as it might sound, that's exactly what I needed to do, to pray myself away from being used by the devil, being used by a man who claimed he loved me, but didn't. I had to show myself that GOD loved me more, that it was time for me to love myself and walk out in faith, that I would be ok, just like I was the last time, and the time before that. I no longer needed to depend on this man for sex or financial stability. I would be ok as long as I walked away and never looked back. I would be ok as long as I took the leap of faith. GOD had already made provisions for me to come out of this addiction. There is power in me that GOD has given me to live with the convictions of my sins and make my wrongs right.

Power in You

Acts 4:31 **"And when they had prayed, the place in which they were gathered together was shaken and they were all filled with the spirit and spoke the word of GOD with boldness."**

G OD gives us all power, but it's what we decide to do with the power that He has given us, that matters. For some the power will lay dormant, and for others, we actually use it. If you want the power of the Holy Spirit, and if you are tired of allowing the devil to use you, then you have to change your routine and immerse yourself in the Word of GOD. I was tired of the same results, thinking that GOD would just change me. I had to decide that I was ready to be changed and use the power that He gave me. I had to ask GOD to use me. Once I was ready to fully go through the healing process and go through the process of allowing GOD to use me, I started to see the power that I had inside of me.

Once you decide that you will surrender and submit to GOD completely, you won't have the desire to do the same sinful things that were destroying you on the inside and on the outside. Yes, that's correct, you are not only destroyed on the inside but also on the outside. While I thought I was looking good on the outside, it wasn't until I surrendered that I really had a glow and understood what my glow was about. The glow wasn't about me, it was more about GOD shining through me and the power that He allowed me to use once I fully surrendered. I had to decide that I no longer would be the mistress. It took me three years of being in this relationship before I decided that I would pray myself out of this relationship. I would always make excuses as to why I wouldn't get out of this relationship that was no good for me. I just thought it was better than the marriage I was in. Using the excuse that it was better than my marriage, made me stay longer in the relationship. I kept hearing GOD's Word, but I wouldn't act on it. Many wonder why they don't hear GOD. It's not that we don't hear Him. It's that we fail to listen and act when we do. I experienced this with this situation. It wasn't until I realized that I no longer had a choice but to act on what I was hearing from GOD. My youngest son always asks me to pray for others. I told my youngest I can't pray over others until I get my life in order. This was one way that GOD was speaking to me. GOD was using my son to communicate to me to get my life in order and surrender. How could I pray over others when I was committing sinful acts that I knew were against the word of GOD? I had to be convicted of this sin. I had to be delivered and the only way that I could do that was to use the power that GOD had given me. There is no way to feel the power if we are not obedient to Him. Being tired and finding fire in my faith, showed me what faith looks like in the darkness. Even though it's dark in our lives when we are living in sin, there is faith that is within us all. We have to activate the faith that lies within us to have the light outshine the darkness that we are going through. Faith is light in the darkness.

Faith is Light in Darkness

Acts 26:18 "to open their eyes, *in order* to turn *them* from darkness to light, and *from* the power of Satan to GOD, that they may receive forgiveness of sins and an inheritance among those who are sanctified by faith in Me"

My experience of adulterous behavior and my marriage showed me that faith is really light in the darkness. Both of these life-changing experiences had me in a dark place. While I assumed that being the mistress was good, it really wasn't. I was in denial as I was engaging in this behavior. I was looking for healing in all the wrong places. This is what adulterous women do unintentionally. We all want to be loved, but at what cost? Is it worth living in the dark for so long that we can't even see what light could be? We must open our eyes and turn from the power of Satan and allow GOD's power in. As the scripture tells us, that we must open our eyes in order to turn the darkness into light. I had to be saved from myself so that I could open my eyes and turn the darkness to light. You may not understand why I say I had to be saved from myself, but I was my own enemy, subjecting myself to sinful, adulterous, sexual behavior. This addiction is no different than any other addiction. I wanted to continue to chase this same feeling every day, all day. My goal was to engage in sexual activity two or three times a day, if I could. I wanted something different. I wanted to change. I knew I wanted a change, but I had to decide that I was ready for this change. I kept using the same old excuse that many use - "Oh GOD knows my heart; He knows that I love Him." Unfortunately, GOD knowing your heart doesn't change the fact that you are still engaging in sinful acts and you really are not asking for forgiveness. You continue with this process and you somehow think that, because He knows your heart, it's ok. As women, we must find a way that we don't subject ourselves to thinking this is ok. Often, we think because we are not caught by their wife, we can continue this behavior. I know that was one of the reasons that I continued. I just felt like, even though I was losing a battle with him not leaving, I was still winning because his wife didn't find out. Listen, we are only fooling ourselves to think, just because his wife doesn't know, we can continue this. No, we can't. This isn't just about his wife. This is about your life. What you deserve and what you don't deserve. You damn sure don't deserve to be living in a dark space because you decided that you will be the mistress. But you must ask yourself, what are you really receiving from this? I received nothing but heartache. I fell in love with a married man that I knew would never be mine. I fell in love with someone who wasn't willing to leave their family. Isn't your mind and body worth more than this? Asking GOD to save me from myself and to allow me to use the power within me directed me, to this scripture. I always referred back to this on my weakest days. I also suggest you use it during your weakest moments.

Romans 8:6 "For to be carnally minded *is* death, but to be spiritually minded *is* life and peace".

I had to always remind myself that I don't have to use my body or allow anyone else to. You don't have to use your body any longer either. I don't have to be in the dark and wonder when the next visit would be. There will be weak days in your transformation and the process of true healing with GOD. But the more that you seek GOD and His Word, and are around bible-believing teaching individuals, the more your life will change. We are seeking the light of truth, to get rid of our sinful lustful deceitful desires. In your transformation you will need to dig deep into your faith, build so you can conquer your rehabilitation. You will use your power to help you in your transformation. Once you start to see the light in your transformation, your darkness will continue to fade, and your faith will start to expand. Your faith will become the light in the darkness.

Power in the Paper

O ne sticky turned into my life. The power of a piece of paper can change your life. Literally. It can help you build a relationship with GOD and change your sinful behavior. You have to decide that you will walk away from what's no good for you, mentally and physically. While we often think what we are into doesn't require change, you can't possibly think your actions won't have consequences.

Any addiction that we become addicted to can destroy us. We all are fighting some type of addiction, every day. The real question is, how do we conquer it?

Six years ago, I started a sticky journal which turned into me building a stronger relationship with GOD than I have ever had. I had to turn to my prayer room and a sticky to conquer my addiction and save my life. For three years I wouldn't ask GOD to deliver me from my addiction and my adulterous behavior. One day I decided that I would finally write on my sticky that I wanted to be delivered. I asked GOD to take this feeling away from me and deliver me from this married man. I no longer wanted to be in a relationship with him, the waiting, the pain, and all that came with it. I was finally ready to be done with it. I started to feel that I was missing what GOD truly had for me. I remember, one morning, walking into my prayer room, writing on a pink highlighted sticky, 'GOD, remove this MARRIED MAN OUT OF MY LIFE.'

So many times, I told this man that I couldn't be with him anymore and he wouldn't go. He would continue to text, call and whatever else he thought would do it. BUT GOD... it was that moment that I wrote it on the sticky that I received a text from him the following day that read:

"Hey Tiff, I have a lot going on right now, so I'm going to fall back. I wish u well in all your future endeavors. You're still cool with me. Friends first"

Matthew 7:7 "Ask and it will be given to you; seek and you will find; knock and the door will be opened to you."

Yes, you are reading correctly, and yes, it was the next day I got this text. I couldn't believe it. I called my girlfriend, so upset. I was like, "Could you believe that this dude actually sent me this text, but didn't have the nerve to call and tell me? But had the nerve to call if he wanted sex!"

But it was at that moment that my girlfriend made me realize what just happened. I asked GOD to remove him, and He did just that. For three years I did not ask, and at the moment of me asking, GOD removed him. He didn't remove him out of my life the way I wanted him to, he moved him by His WILL. Talk about the power of GOD! If this doesn't make you change your life, then I don't know what will!!! Often, we want GOD to answer our prayers the way we want Him to, and not how GOD wants to. Sit still for a moment. I used my power that GOD gave me to pray this man out of my life, to finally get rid of my addictions and my sinful behavior. See, you might not get this, but GOD's power is real. I never wanted to pray out of it because I knew GOD would take me out of it. So, when I decided that I would, GOD did just that!! Gone. Over. Out. This man sent me a text the next day!! I was hurt. I couldn't believe it.

The power of the sticky.

The power of GOD.

Do you hear me? Do you see what GOD will do? Do you understand that He will save you from yourself and your addictions? I was finally tired. I was finally fed up, and GOD saved me. GOD answered my prayer and saved me from myself. What makes you think He won't do the same for you? You are no different than I. We are all GOD's children.

This is no longer about me. This is about you. You have had the opportunity to go through my valleys and my mountains in this memoir. While some may read this as, "Oh, it's just another story, like all the rest," no, it's not like all the rest. It's mine, and I OWN it, every bit of it, and one day you will have to own yours. You may even have to resist this text one more time. Understand, I wrote in a sticky, "GOD remove this married man," and this is what I GOT. I didn't edit the text; I didn't change it. But what I did do was save it, so that I would always know how GOD saved me.

"Hey Tiff, I have a lot going on right now, so I'm going to fall back. I wish u well in all your future endeavors. You're still cool with me. Friends first"

I never imagined that writing my prayers on a highlighted sticky would change my life in so many ways. Each and every prayer that I wrote on the sticky has been answered.

Luke 6:12 "And it came to pass in those days, that he went out into a mountain to pray, and continued all night in prayer to GOD"

The question you must ask yourself is, are you ready for this powerful change of a sticky? I am winning all the way! I use pen and paper to build my relationship with GOD and He answers me. How could I not love Him for not only delivering me from my mess, but saving me from myself. I have been very transparent with you because, let me help you understand, you can't heal what you don't reveal. Are you ready to heal? Aren't you tired of that life? Start healing honey, and start allowing GOD to love you. His love is unconditional. Reveal what you are ready to heal.

Can't Heal What You Don't Reveal

I was walking around like a zombie, wondering when I would shake this feeling. You are still feeling crazy, trying to figure out how long you will teeter-totter with GOD. You see a little light and you think it's a blessing, until the next storm comes blazing though your life. Then you start to question yourself and your actions. You go back and forth, trying to decide if you will stay being the mistress, or you will end it.

Ma'am, you can't heal what you don't reveal to yourself or others. Walking around in the hall of shame weighs heavy on you. There is no way that you are living peacefully. There is no way that you are even sleeping at this point. You are confused. You want to throw in the towel, but you haven't quite figured out how to truly love yourself, and you are scared that you are going to be alone. Ma'am let me give you the news that you already know. You are alone and have been alone the whole time while you have been the mistress. Leave him. He isn't going to leave you or the wife. You have to be in control of your life. Conviction has already occurred, and you have ignored it for some time. Reveal, so that you can heal. Get it out, scream it out. Get around other women that will help you. Your true girlfriends won't encourage you to sleep with someone's husband. Start healing so that you know how to love. It's time for you to love 'you'. NO, I am not telling you that you don't need a man. But what I am saying to you is, you don't need another woman's man. He can do nothing for you. And this isn't about bashing a man. This is about healing yourself. This is about finding the love of GOD so that you are able to love the man GOD has for you. So that man that GOD has for you will be able to love you. You can be REDEEMED. I am REDEEMED. I am not my past and you don't have to be yours.

LET GO AND LET GOD. You think this was a big secret, but it was never a secret, because he was never leaving his wife. The real secret was, he was never going to make you his woman. You never wanted to face it because you thought one day that he was going to belong to you. Sis, it's time for you to HEAL, to become sound and healthy again. It's time for you to alleviate the distress and anguish. I am renewed, restored and rejuvenated, but most of all, GOD SAVED ME FROM MYSELF. Are you ready to be saved from yourself? Reveal this to yourself. Get out of denial. It's time; it's long overdue. Sis, you owe this to yourself. Reveal it so you can heal it. You are more than a conqueror. GOD will forgive you, but are you ready to forgive yourself?

Psalm 103:2-5 "Who forgives all your iniquities,

Who heals all your diseases,

Who redeems your life from destruction,

Who crowns you with loving kindness and tender mercies,

Who satisfies your mouth with good *things,*

***So that* your youth is renewed like the eagle's."**

Forgiveness

ealing your past begins with forgiving completely. It starts with you, Sis. You have to forgive yourself. You are probably wondering why I am telling you to forgive yourself. Yes, you were the problem. You engaged with someone's husband and you didn't see an issue with it, because you allowed yourself to be in a relationship with him. I am not judging you, but what I am saying is, cut the cord. Love you, forgive you, hug you. Spend some time with you. Figure out who you are. Use this time of forgiveness to move on and find out what the root of the problem is. There is a reason why you feel the need to sleep with someone's husband. Trust me, I know. I have been there. For me it was several factors and one was generational curse. The other was, I thought I got away with it and I didn't want the attachment. So I thought, until I fell in love. Forgive yourself for staying in it so long. Forgive yourself for not loving yourself and taking care of you. You were so focused on taking care of him, you forgot about yourself. You may have thought you were taking care of you because you got dressed up every time you went to meet him. You did all the things he liked. You put on the stilettos, you put on the skirt with no panties and the finest perfume. I get it. Trust me, I do. All of the above was my ritual every time I seen him. That wasn't for you. That was for him. Break those chains, Sis. They have been weighing you down for too long. The entire cycle has mentally and physically tried to break you, but you are still here. You may have been gracefully broken in some capacity, but GOD is a saving GOD, a forgiving GOD and a loving GOD. You are freeing yourself by forgiving yourself.

Luke 7:47-48 "Therefore I say to you, her sins, which are many, are forgiven, for she loved much. But to whom little is forgiven, the same loves little."

Forgiveness opens the door to your blessings. You have to not only forgive yourself, but you have to forgive the man that you allowed into your space when you knew that he would never be your man. You settled. You accepted it, so now you can't be mad because it's over. You have to forgive him and never pick up the phone or ever look back again, because you knew what you got yourself into when he told you he was married, or even if he didn't tell you first, and you found out.

FORGIVE. GOD forgave you the moment you asked for forgiveness. Walking around with an unforgiving heart and mind will kill you Sis. Haven't you already been through enough? How long did you stay in the relationship, or are you still in it? You are more than a mistress. You are ENOUGH. You don't have to be the other woman. You won't have to hide the confessions or hold them. You can be redeemed! GOD's grace is unmatched, and His spiritual powers will change you.

His Grace - My Grind

James 2:26 " For as the body without the spirit is dead, so faith without works is dead also."

Many times, I have told you, and I have spoken on GOD saving me from myself. While some may still not understand this, many will. GOD tells us that faith without works is dead. In my transgressions and sinful behavior, I mentioned how my world was also surrounded by money. I would not sleep with any man, married or not, without money. This all came to a halt when I decided that I would surrender and submit to GOD. I had to give up everything that came along with my sex addiction. When I asked GOD to deliver me from the married man and the relationship, that meant I had to also ask GOD to deliver me from the financial part of it as well. Growing up in the generational curse I was always told, 'You walk with a moneymaker every day and you shouldn't be broke, ever'. Well I took that and ran with it, along with my sex addiction. If you weren't paying, you weren't slaying, and that was literally. No way would I sleep with someone, make them feel great, and I walk away with nothing. That was understood from the beginning.

After, GOD answered my prayers immediately. I had walked away from everything - the man, and the money. Several times he called, and I would ignore it, or he would text, and I would ignore it. Several times he would send me his bank statement so that I would give in. He thought that the money would bring me back. But, keep in mind, he sent the text, so in reality he was also used by GOD and didn't even know it. You send me a text saying you have to fall back, but a week or two later, you are calling and texting. GOD stepped in. It didn't happen, not once after I gave up, and GOD answered my prayers and delivered me. I walked away. Walking away completely meant there were no extra funds. There were no lavish handbags, traveling would be far and few and the expensive jewelry would be no more. I was working full-time and I was able to take care of myself, but it was the greed that would no longer be, and I was finally ok with that. How could I not be, when this is what I finally had the courage to ask for and get out. This would mean that I had to step my prayer life up, and my relationship with GOD up more. This is where I had to totally put my faith on an elevated level. I regrouped and decided if I wanted these items that this man was giving me, I had to grind harder. I had to apply GOD's Grace and my grind. I knew, with the two, I would be just fine. And that's what I have been. My girlfriends always used to say, 'You don't need his money. You are able to take care of yourself.' But how could I see that when I was already blind? Living in that life meant everything was a blur. And when I tell you that, that's just what I mean. I was getting money from him but because I was in a sinful life, GOD made it so that it wouldn't even last. I started grinding more than ever. This was something I had to do for the healing process. Getting a second job not only took my mind and thoughts away from recovering from my sex addition, but it put me in another mindset. I was able to grind and be free. The chains started to fall more and more each day. I was able to spend time in the word of GOD and spend time with Tiffany. This is what GOD had me to do. He had me turn my grind into focusing on who He was and what He would do for me. GOD's Grace, and my grind, changed my life forever.

My body was no longer a source of income. Yes, you read that right. My body was a source of my income. I relied on that income. I didn't have to work hard; it was something I thought I enjoyed. But GOD, when I asked Him to deliver me, He did just that. He turned my second source income into hard labor work. He made me grind. He made me focus on who He was and what He had for me. This was all part of the process of GOD forgiving me, teaching me that if you grind for what you want, you will have My Grace. You won't have to destroy your temple to please what doesn't belong to you. At what price are you willing to make this sacrifice? What are you willing to walk away from to gain what GOD has for you? I gave it all up. I surrendered each day. I turned the Grace He gave me into a grind, and I can't begin to tell you the doors that have opened for me. Never have I tried to pretend to be perfect but what I do know is, His Grace and my grind changed my path.

In all of this my pain made me pray and my prayer made me powerful. You read the text. I didn't make it up. I asked GOD to remove me from the married man and he answered the next day. That wasn't just a small prayer; that was a loaded prayer. Not only did He remove me from the married man, He healed me in the process. He changed me in the process, and He is using me in the process. I stand available to be used and, not by man, but by GOD. Allow GOD's Grace and your grind to transform you. Those expensive bags you want? Save up. Trust me, it will be more rewarding. And if you are anything like me, you are probably not even carrying them. When you are free you will see none of that materialistic crap matters anymore. You are looking for a spiritual high, not a materialistic one. You are looking to have JOY – it's internal and will be visible externally. Happiness is temporary. Joy is everlasting. Allow His Grace over you. GOD wants to use you so that you are working for Him. Your faith is dead without the works.

Pain made me pray and prayer made me powerful.

How powerful is it to write on a piece of paper, and GOD responds in twenty-four hours? I was always scared to pray this man out of my life. I always had a feeling GOD would release me, but I didn't want it. Everyone would always ask me to pray for them, or with them, but I didn't feel comfortable doing it because I wasn't living right. How could I even think about praying with someone, for them or over them, for that matter? How would GOD answer their prayers if I am not living right? Me praying for them would be a spiritual connection. I would pray for years with my girlfriends, so much that they would call me Deacon Thomas. I used to tell them, "No, don't put that on me, or call me that. I am not living right." But what does that really mean - I am not living right? I can't pray? Of course not. What this life has taught me was that I had to pray the totally opposite, and pray some more. I had to pray my pain away. I had to start praying for myself. I had to ask GOD to deliver me. I had to focus on GOD and what he would do with me. I have seen what the fire looks like. It was time for me to really experience what GOD had for me. I went to WAR. Literally, war against myself. The more I prayed, the more GOD heard my cry. I cried, I screamed, and I prayed some more. I fasted and I prayed, and I am telling you, GOD delivered me from myself.

Luke 9:23 "Then He said to *them* all, "If anyone desires to come after Me, let him deny himself, and take up his cross daily, and follow Me."

I know what it's like to walk through the fire, but I never really knew what it was like to burn for GOD. I wanted that love that GOD gave me when I couldn't give it to myself. I chased the wrong thing for too many years, and it almost destroyed me. I am not ashamed; I am not embarrassed, and I am not hiding. GOD told me to walk very BOLDLY. GOD said, "Stand up my child, I have delivered you and you are now on the battlefield for me. You are to go out in the world and tell everyone who you are, because you are redeemed and you know the power that GOD has given you."

You can also have the same power. We all have some pain that we go through that will make us feel that we are powerless. You have to use your pain to make you powerful. You could possibly be reading this and responding, "No way". But I am here, telling you that I prayed my way out of my hell. You are no different than I am. Sis, pray your way out of your hell. Pray yourself away from that man. Let him GO. Pray for his family, pray for his wife. Pray that GOD repairs their marriage. You are saving yourself by doing this. This is the time GOD can use your flesh. Allow GOD to use your flesh for healing. This is what this adulterous life is really about - your flesh. You are fighting your flesh. Get out now before it costs you everything. You have to ask yourself, "Is it worth me losing everything? Is it worth him losing everything?" I recall after one of many sexual encounters, the married man asked me if his wife found out, would I be willing to allow him to move in with me. The answer to him was 'NO'. I answered 'no' because, as soon as his wife decided to take him back, guess what, he would be gone. That fast, he would go right back to her. No way was I willing to encounter that, and that was another wake-up call for me. How many wake-up calls do you need? Do you need me to go down the list of what GOD has probably already saved you from? Yes, that just made you think right. Go to war with yourself. Yes, that might sound crazy, but that's what you need to do to be delivered. You have to fight the other 'you'. I had to fight the weak Tiffany. I had to let her know that she couldn't have me anymore, that I was allowing GOD to have me. You have to stand up against your alter ego. Think about it, who else are you standing up to? I won the war!! The battle is over. It's been almost a year since I have had any sexual encounters because I decided that I would no longer allow my flesh to win, nor would I use my body for the wrong reasons. I escaped, and you can escape too. Yes, that's what it is, escaping everything that was meant to destroy you. Yes, you were wrong. Yes, it was a sin, but you are asking GOD to deliver you. You are asking GOD to forgive you. You are asking GOD to go to war for you. You won't be able to do this alone. You will need GOD's armor. Put on the belt of truth, the breastplate of righteousness, get your feet fitted with the gospel of peace, the shield of faith, your helmet of salvation and the sword of the Spirit, and fight like hell. There will be many things that you have to do differently, but you will love yourself in the end. Every day I fight the sex addiction because it never goes away, but I fight it with GOD. I allow GOD to fight for me now. I just stand out of the way and allow His Will. You might not understand what I am saying, or you might. I am here for you Sis.

Isaiah 43:2 "When you pass through the waters, I *will be* with you; And through the rivers, they shall not overflow you. When you walk through the fire, you shall not be burned, Nor shall the flame scorch you".

GOD TAUGHT ME HOW TO PRAY and he can do the same for you. Drop down on your knees and this time, not for man, but for GOD.

Equally Yoked

Dear GOD,

You saved me from myself. When I had no hope, you were the only hope I had. When nothing was left in me, you rescued me. You showed me what love feels like, what it looks like. I am thankful that when I walked out of the fire, I asked you to show me and teach me. I asked you to use me and, while you do, protect me. And for that I am thankful, I am grateful and blessed. You showed me how important it is to depend on you. You showed me that no matter what lies ahead of me, you are already ahead of them. While most of my foolishness was self-inflicted, you still gave me another chance. I don't proclaim to be perfect at all, but I am faithful. I didn't know what faithful was before I surrendered, before I submitted to you. But now I know what it means. You are teaching me faithfulness, you are teaching me forgiveness, you are teaching me unconditional love. Thank you for your deliverance. I thought that there was no way out of the fire when the fire was flaming, but I walked out without being burned. I walked out without being scorched. I was able to walk through the waters and not drown. You delivered me from adulterous behavior, sex addiction, and abuse.

Another one of my prayers to GOD was for Him to allow me to walk into my next relationship with someone that was equally yoked with me. For someone to help me get to my next level with GOD. This is very important to me and should be equally important to you. I want my next relationship to have GOD in the beginning, middle, and end. Let me tell you, as many of my prayers GOD answered, He also answered that one. I met a GOD-fearing man in my walk. When I tell you this is different, this is different! When you ask GOD for something, know that He will give it to you, but will you be ready when He does? This man has helped elevate my walk with GOD, and my spiritual walk. While I thought I would bring my past into this relationship by trying to have a sexual encounter, GOD stopped me in my tracks. Remember, I told you, the sex addiction is real and just like any addiction, I am still fighting it every day. I asked this man if he would have sex and he rejected me. Yes, you heard me. He told me 'No'. He said, "If you are not willing to be my wife then, no." You see, that's *POWER*. I have never ever been rejected. I thought I had power to have sex with anyone and whoever, but I ran up against the Holy Ghost. I asked him a few times and every time I got the same answer. He told me five minutes of pleasure wasn't worth losing the love that GOD has for me or him. Talk about power and GOD giving you what you ask for at the same time. Come on through GOD. At that moment, and each moment thereafter, when I asked, I knew GOD was using him, as this is what I asked GOD for.

So you see, I have given you all the tools and all the ways that GOD delivered me. The blueprint is here. I asked GOD to help me with this for you. Now the rest is up to you. All you have to do is decide that you won't be ashamed; you won't be scared to be transparent; you won't be scared to seek GOD. You have the same courage that I do. My faith calmed the storms and your faith can do the same. My pain was for a purpose, which has turned into my passion of healing others. I have seen the supernatural that GOD has given to me. Let go!! Let GOD find your way. I know that there is power in persistent prayer.

Micah 7:7 "Therefore I will look to the LORD; I will wait for the GOD of my salvation; My GOD will hear me."

We live in a world of self-inflicted pain believing that the devil has more for us then GOD. Our GOD is GOD of Process, something in you that GOD is hatching by the circumstance around you. Your victory is tied to your thought life. I am spiritually awakened, and I am Redeemed. You are no different than I and no circumstance that you are in is too big for the King. GOD's promises are true. Get in the posture to be delivered. I stand awakened as I BOLDLY walk in the Will of GOD. Come and walk with me. This is my EXODUS. GOD forgave me and, in turn, I was able to forgive myself. Because of His Grace and Mercy, it's my divine order to spread the gospel and help free the damage and brokenness of all the other Tiffanies. It's your turn to be free. It's your turn to be free!

Psalm 46:5 "GOD *is* in the midst of her, she shall not be moved; GOD shall help her, just at the break of dawn."

I have nothing to defend. I have nothing to protect. I have nothing to prove. I am #TIFFANYDAVISSPEAKS and I am *FREE*.

Tiffany A. Davis

Tiffany A. Davis

www.ingramcontent.com/pod-product-compliance
Lightning Source LLC
Chambersburg PA
CBHW021338090426
42742CB00008B/651